LOCOMOTIVES
in detail

RIDDLES CLASS 6/7 | **5** | **STANDARD PACIFICS**

LOCOMOTIVES

in detail

RIDDLES CLASS 6/7   **STANDARD PACIFICS**

DAVID CLARKE

Ian Allan
PUBLISHING

I am old enough to not only see most of the 'Britannias' (I only missed out on seeing three of the class, No. 70002 *Geoffrey Chaucer*, No. 70007 *Coeur-de-Lion*, and No. 70039 *Sir Christopher Wren*) but also to have been pulled by them on a number of occasions. When I visited Crewe Works in February 1965 I was pulled from Birmingham New Street by No. 70042 *Lord Roberts* into the works and on visits to the two Crewe Depots on the same day I saw a total of 21 'Britannias' and unusually one 'Clan' (at Crewe North). The last time I was pulled by one of the class was in September 1966 when I travelled on the only Class 1 train on the West Coast main line to be rostered for steam when I caught the Barrow to Euston train at Preston and travelled to Crewe (where steam was replaced by electric) behind No. 70011 *Hotspur* (running with painted name) The locomotive may not have been particularly clean but was in good mechanical condition and gave me a good run to Crewe. Even at the stage where the steam fleet was being run down they were capable of good performance. Although they were now in their dull plain khaki green livery they were still imposing locomotives and were capable of hauling anything the operating department threw at them. From 1964 onwards they were the mainstay of the West Coast route in terms of steam and were used on any train from unfitted mineral up to express passenger, a fitting tribute to their 7MT (mixed traffic) capability.

I also have a family connection with the 'Britannias' as my younger brother; Phillip, is a qualified steam locomotive driver and fired No. 70000 *Britannia* many times when it worked on the Nene Valley Railway (Peterborough) in the 1980s.

The 'Britannias' from a detail point of view are deceptively complex with many of the detail changes being very subtle and not always easy to spot in photographs. The Engine History Cards have been analysed but as with other classes the cards suffer from not being updated from 1964 onwards so many of the later changes (such as tenders) were not officially recorded. So for many of the latter changes I have used an extensive collection of photographs and observations from such sources as the *Railway Observer*. Where I have used previously published lists for

changes and variants I have validated this with photographic evidence and where the photograph contradicts the published data I have not used the published sources. In the course of doing the research for the book I came across a number of contradictory statements, sometimes within the same book (including dates two years different for the date a name was applied!) so if there are any errors they are mine not a simple reiteration of 'facts' from an unknown source.

Where a locomotive number is used the name will always follow. Even at the point where the locomotives no longer carried names I will use the name also.

Producing a book is not a solitary process; a number of people have provided help and assistance in me producing this book. The detail shots of *Britannia* were taken at Barrow Hill Roundhouse, and my thanks go to Mervyn Allcock for arranging access when the shed was not open to the public.

Also thanks to Geoff Sharpe who had a search through his files to find me the additional photographs I required. Also I am grateful to Mike Peascod for the use of his excellent and detailed drawings of the class.

David Clarke
Derby, March 2006

Bibliography
BR Standard Steam Locomotives Volume 1. RCTS. This is an extensive reference source and is recommended.
Britannia. Phillip Atkins. Irwell Press 1991. An excellent book now long out of print and commanding very high prices, and very difficult to find.
The Book of the Britannia Pacifics. Irwell Press 2004.
Britannia Pacifics. Gavin Morrison and Peter Swinger. Ian Allan 2003.
BR Standard Pacifics. Peter Swinger. Ian Allan 1994.
Locomotive Panorama Volume 1. E S Cox. Ian Allan 1966. This gives an authoritative insight into the development and production of the Standard classes from someone who was intimately involved in the process and decision making. Strongly recommended.

Photograph Credits
Colour-Rail (CR) and their photographers
P. M. Alexander (PA); K. Bannister (KB);
Alan Chandler, MBE (AC); M. Chapman (MC);
I. Davidson (ID); J. Davenport (JD); R. Denison (RD);
P. J. Fritton (PJF); P. Glenn (PGL); Gordon Green (GG);
C. C. B. Herbert (CCH); P. J. Hughes (PHu);
Historical Model Railway Society (HMR); R. P. Jackson (RPJ);
D. A. Kelso (DAK); Roger Kingshott (RK); J. B. McCann (JMc);
J. Mitchell (DJM); J. H. Moss (JM); W. O. Oliver (WO);
T. B. Owen (TO); Pursey C. Short (PCS); M. Smith (MS);
Douglas Tritton (DCT); S. C. Townroe (ST); S. M. Watkins (SW);
P. H. Wells (PHW).
Authors Collection (AC).
Ian Allan Library (IA) and photographers
R. Atkins (RA); V. Bamford (VB); I. S. Carr (ISC);
J. R. Carter (JRC); A. J. Clarke (AJC); C. R. L. Coles (CRLC);
John Corkhill (JC); A. W. Flowers (AWF); P. Gerald (PG);
Ian C. Gumm (ICG); G. F. Heiron (GFH); K. P. Laurence (KPL);
P. L. Simpson (PLS); J. R. Smith (JRS).

Series Created & Edited by Jasper Spencer-Smith.
Design and artwork: Nigel Pell.
Produced by JSS Publishing Limited, P.O. Box 6031, Bournemouth, Dorset, England.
Colour scanning: JPS Limited, Branksome, Poole, Dorset BH12 1DJ

Title spread:
No. 70024 *Vulcan* passing Reading West main signal box with the 13.55 Paddington to Pembroke Dock service, May 1958. (CR/WO)

First published 2006

ISBN (10) 0 7110 3177 0
ISBN (13) 978 0 7110 3177 7

Published by Ian Allan Publishing

an imprint of Ian Allan Publishing Ltd, Hersham, Surrey KT12 4RG.
Printed in England by Ian Allan Printing Ltd, Hersham, Surrey KT12 4RG.

Code: 0606/B2

Visit the Ian Allan Publishing website at www.ianallanpublishing.com

INTRODUCTION
PAGE 6

CHAPTER ONE
DESIGN
PAGE 10

CHAPTER TWO
CONSTRUCTION
PAGE 22

CHAPTER THREE
LIVERIES & NAMES
PAGE 46

CHAPTER FOUR
IN SERVICE
PAGE 62

CHAPTER FIVE
THE CLANS
PAGE 80

CHAPTER SIX
PRESERVATION
PAGE 88

APPENDICES
DRAWINGS
PAGE 90

INTRODUCTION

The question of which Standard class to be built first was driven by operating considerations. The most pressing need was for a Class 7 on the Great Eastern section of the Eastern Region.

With the formation of British Railways on 1 January 1948 a new strategy was required for the forward direction of motive power and the issue could be distilled into two options:

1. Allow the newly formed regions (based very much on the former Big Four companies) to continue to design and build their own designs, independently of the other regions.
2. Develop a range of 'Standard' locomotives that could run on any of the regions and which would incorporate best practice, not only from within the UK but from the rest of the world, particularly from the USA.

At the end of the war a number of senior engineers from the LMS and LNER went to the USA to study railway practice and the nine leading railroads were visited.

It became clear almost immediately that the preferred option would be to design a range of standard steam locomotives and to stop building the former railway company designs. One of the principle reasons behind this decision was to reduce both the cost of building and the cost of operating. In the post-war period there was recognition that there would be labour shortages in the area of locomotive maintenance and that any new designs should incorporate these principles.

However it would take time to design these new locomotives and for a short period some existing designs continued to be built to fill the gap; these included the ex-LNER 'A1' class 4-6-2s (21 built) and ex-LMS Black 5 class (40 built). A total of 1,538 locomotives of Big Four designs were built after the formation of British Railways and before the BR Standards were introduced.

As a precursor to the production of any standard designs and to assist in the design process, locomotive trials were arranged in 1948 where the most modern locomotives in a number of categories were run on other regions and comparisons made on some key criteria: average and maximum power, also coal consumption.

The list of standard locomotives had four completely new designs (including the 'Britannia'), four new designs based on existing types and four using existing designs with only minor modifications. The decision on which to proceed with first was driven by operating considerations, the most pressing need was for a Class 7 to improve services on the Great Eastern section of the Eastern Region, so the 'Britannias' became the first of the standard class locomotives to enter service.

There are many who questioned the wisdom of designing a new range of locomotives rather than continue to build designs from the former companies but this does not form the *raison d'etre* of this book.

Above:
No 70043 at Rugby, March 1954. It is fitted with Westinghouse air-braking pumps. Plain rods are fitted with the original LNER-style crank fixing. (CR/JMc)

Left:
No. 70047, the only unnamed locomotive in the class, passing through Leyland with an up freight. It retains original style smoke deflectors and is AWS fitted. (CR/RK)

No. 70010 *Owen Glendower* at Crewe South in June 1967 with the blower on to generate more steam. No. 70010 is fitted with the modified smoke deflectors and is also equipped with a speedometer. The locomotive appears to be in good condition although was soon to be withdrawn from service in September 1967. (DC)

Above:
No. 70050 *Firth of Clyde* at Annersley depot (Nottingham), in late 1965. (IA/AJC)

Left:
No. 70014 *Iron Duke* at Carlisle (Kingmoor) in October 1966. Note, the different coupling rods and that no front numberplate is fitted. No. 70014 is coupled to BR1 tender but by January 1967 it had a BR1D tender. (IA/KPL)

CHAPTER ONE

DESIGN

The design of the BR Standard classes was intended
to take the best practice, not only from the
previous companies but also from foreign railways.

In 1948 the newly formed British Railways set up a design team under R. A. 'Robin' Riddles to design and build a range of 'standard' steam locomotives to fill the gap before the railway network was electrified. The design of the BR Standard classes was intended to take the best practice not only from the previous companies but also from foreign practice. During World War Two some of the features of the US-built 'S160' class 2-8-0s (running on the British network prior to moving to the Continent) attracted some attention with the use of rocker ash pans and self cleaning smoke boxes to make disposal easier and quicker. Also some of the principals in the design team had also travelled abroad and had been influenced by what they had seen. The LMS led the way after the war with H. A. Ivatt (the LMS Chief Mechanical Engineer) incorporating self cleaning smoke boxes, rocker ash pans, manganese bearings and roller bearings in the last LMS designs and many of these features were incorporated into the new BR Standard class designs. Also best practice from the pre-nationalised companies was also considered. Each design in the range was allocated a drawing office which took primary responsibility for the design, but which also had to use components from a standard list.

Derby was the lead for the design of the 'Britannia' (and subsequently the 'Clan') initially under the guidance of T. F. Coleman who had carried out a similar job for Sir William Stanier and Ivatt (and therefore had been responsible for all the locomotives introduced under those august engineers) but Coleman retired in 1949 and was replaced by C. S. Cocks who came from the Southern Railway (SR). However, Derby was only responsible for the overall design and many of the major components were designed at Brighton, Doncaster and Swindon.

The key features on the 'Britannia' were as follows:

1. The horn guides for the axleboxes were located in the centre of the frames making the frames closer together, this had been developed by Bulleid for the 'Merchant Navy' class and the intention was to produce a set of frames that would be resistant to cracking.

2. The use of 6ft 2in (1.88m) driving wheels for a Pacific. This followed the practice first seen on the SR 'West Country' class and the LNER 'A2' Pacifics both using 6ft 2in (1.88m) driving wheels, without adversely affecting high-speed performance and giving better mixed traffic capability.

3. The use of two cylinders on a Pacific type locomotive. All previous contemporary designs (such as the LNER 'A2' and SR

Above:
No 70000 *Britannia* at Shrewsbury in the 1960s. The locomotive is fitted with plain rods and LMS-style smoke deflectors. Note the lowered vacuum pipe on the buffer beam. (DC)

Left:
No 70047 being readied for the 'Irish Mail' service at Holyhead, August 1959. The locomotive is fitted with the original type of smoke deflectors and is coupled to a BR1D tender. (CR/HMR)

Top:
No. 70000 *Britannia*
as built 1951 in plain
black livery, a few
weeks before being
repainted BR Green
and named. (DC)

Above:
No. 70000 *Britannia*
as running in October
1964 with many of
the modifications
applied to the class.
The rods are now
plain, the return crank
has a four-bolt fixing
and there are no
holes in the axles.
AWS and speedo-
meter are fitted. (DC)

'Merchant Navy') all used three cylinders, but two cylinders had benefits in cost of construction and more importantly in reduced maintenance and locomotive preparation. The cylinders were the largest that could be accommodated within the loading gauge and followed the latest thoughts on steam flow with large straight ports, large diameter and long travel piston valves, all with the specific intention of ensuring maximum cylinder efficiency. The slide bar and crosshead arrangement followed LNER (and SR 'Merchant Navy' class) practice.

4. The cab and footplating was suspended from the boiler (not on the frames) and the cab floor extended back under the tender coal shute giving a single floor to stand on in contrast to the arrangements where there was

a fall plate between tender footplate and locomotive footplate.

5. A high running plate which avoided the need for wheel splashers, saving weight and making maintenance easier.

Much thought went into the design of the cab and operating controls with a full-size mock up being constructed for assessment by driving staff.

The 'Britannia' boiler was one of four new wide firebox boilers designed for the new Standard classes (the other three being the 'Clan', the *Duke of Gloucester* and the '9F'), the other Standard classes utilising boilers based on existing companies (the BR Standard Class 5 using a boiler essentially the same as the LMS Class 5).

Following post-war Southern Railway practice the firebox was fitted with a rocking

grate which enabled the fireman to break up clinker and allow ash to fall into the ash pan whilst the locomotive was in motion. The ash pans were fitted with bottom doors (following post war LMS practice) enabling the ash pan to be emptied by using an external lever making disposal much easier (and safer as the disposal staff did not need to use fire irons to rake out clinker).

Unusually for a Pacific in the post war era it was fitted with a single chimney (although some of the last Peppercorn 'A2' Pacifics also only had a single chimney) This resulted from the scientific approach to blast pipe design carried out by S.O. Ell at Swindon who showed that better results could be obtained from a well designed single chimney than some of the previous double chimney arrangements.

The use of a multiple-valve regulator in the smokebox followed late LNER practice (fitted to a small number of the 'A2' Pacifics) and also US practice which manifested itself by the regulator rod on the outside of the boiler and the raised access plate behind the chimney.

The wheels were spoked and cast from steel with balancing weights formed by steel plates sandwiching the spokes and riveted through from front to back following LMS practice.

The trailing truck followed Southern Railway practice and was based on the Bulleid Pacifics being fabricated (rather than cast) but with changes to the springing from the SR design. The trailing truck subsequently proved not to be as good as expected and it was surprising that the cast design used on the last two 'Duchess'-class locomotives for the LMS was not used.

Above:
No 70000 *Britannia* at Neasden before being moved to Marylebone for the naming ceremony and inspection. (CR/CCH)

Right:
No 70037 *Hereward the Wake* at March (Cambridgeshire) shed in March 1961. Plain connecting rods are fitted as is a speedometer. Note the LMS-style smoke deflectors and black axlebox covers on the trailing truck and tenders, also the LMS-type four stud fixing for the crank. (CR/ GG)

BR Number	Name	Date Built	Original Tender	Original Coupling Rods	AWS	Speedometer (Smith Stone type)	Withdrawn
No. 70000	*Britannia*	1/1951	BR1	Fluted	Yes (9/1959)	Yes	28/6/1966
No. 70001	*Lord Hurcomb*	2/1951	BR1	Fluted	Yes (9/1959)	Yes	30/8/1966
No. 70002	*Geoffrey Chaucer*	3/1951	BR1	Fluted	Yes (2/1960)	Yes	14/1/1967
No. 70003	*John Bunyan*	3/1951	BR1	Fluted	Yes (3/1957)	Yes	25/03/1967
No. 70004	*William Shakespeare*	3/1951	BR1	Fluted	Never fitted	Never Fitted	30/12/1967.
No. 70005	*John Milton*	4/1951	BR1	Fluted	Yes (5/1959)	Yes	29/07/1967
No. 70006	*Robert Burns*	4/1951	BR1	Fluted	Yes (9/1960)	Yes	20/05/1967
No. 70007	*Coeur-de-Lion*	4/1951	BR1	Fluted	Yes (4/1959)	Yes	19/06/1965
No. 70008	*Black Prince*	4/1951	BR1	Fluted	Yes (10/1959)	Yes	14/01/1967
No. 70009	*Alfred the Great*	5/1951	BR1	Fluted	Yes (6/1959)	Yes	21/01/1967

Left:
No 70046 before naming as *Anzac* at Willesden shed. The locomotive is not fitted with AWS but does have a speedometer. Note the lowered vacuum pipe, modified front step and the lowered top lamp bracket on the smokebox door. (CR/ MS)

Left:
No 70009 *Alfred the Great,* new in ex-works condition at Branksome turntable,1951. The locomotive was temporarily allocated to the Southern Region. (CR/ ST)

BR Number	Name	Date Built	Original Tender	Original Coupling Rods	AWS	Speedometer (Smith Stone type)	Withdrawn
No. 70010	Owen Glendower	5/1951	BR1	Fluted	Yes (9/1959)	Yes	23/09/1967
No. 70011	Hotspur	5/1951	BR1	Fluted	Yes (4/1960)	Yes	23/11/1967
No. 70012	John of Gaunt	5/1951	BR1	Fluted	Yes 10/1960)	Yes	30/12/1967
No. 70013	Oliver Cromwell	5/1951	BR1	Fluted	Yes (5/1959)	Yes	17/08/1968
No. 70014	Iron Duke	6/1951	BR1	Fluted	Yes (2/1963)	Yes	30/12/1967
No. 70015	Apollo	6/1951	BR1	Fluted	Never Fitted	Yes	05/08/1967
No. 70016	Ariel	6/1951	BR1	Fluted	Never fitted	Never fitted	19/08/1967
No. 70017	Arrow	6/1951	BR1	Fluted	Never fitted	Yes	01/10/1966
No. 70018	Flying Dutchman	6/1951	BR1	Fluted	Yes (1/1963)	Yes	24/12/1966
No. 70019	Lightning	6/1951	BR1	Fluted	Never Fitted	Never fitted	12/03/1966

Above:
No. 70021 *Morning Star* at Crewe in August 1951, fitted to a BR1 tender. The step on top of the tank at the rear of the tender has yet to be fitted. The lids on the sandboxes are still level with the top of the footplate. (DC)

BR Number	Name	Date Built	Original Tender	Original Coupling Rods	AWS	Speedometer (Smith Stone type)	Withdrawn
No. 70020	*Mercury*	7/1951	BR1	Fluted	Never Fitted	Yes	21/01/1967
No. 70021	*Morning Star*	8/1951	BR1A	Fluted	Never Fitted	Yes	30/12/1967
No. 70022	*Tornado*	8/1951	BR1A	Fluted	Never Fitted	Never Fitted	23/12/1967
No. 70023	*Venus*	8/1951	BR1A	Fluted	Never fitted	Never fitted	30/12/1967
No. 70024	*Vulcan*	10/1951	BR1A	Fluted	Never fitted	Never Fitted	30/12/1967
No. 70025	*Western Star*	9/1952	BR1A	Plain	Yes (12/1962)	Never Fitted	23/12/1967
No. 70026	*Polar Star*	10/1952	BR1A	Plain	Never Fitted	Yes	14/01/1967
No. 70027	*Royal Star*	10/1952	BR1A	Plain	Never fitted	Never fitted	01/07/1967
No. 70028	*Rising Star*	10/1952	BR1A	Plain	Never Fitted	Never fitted	16/09/1967
No. 70029	*Shooting Star*	11/1952	BR1A	Plain	Yes	Never Fitted	21/10/1967
No. 70030	*William Wordsworth*	11/1952	BR1	Plain	Yes (1/1959)	Yes	25/06/1966
No. 70031	*Byron*	11/1952	BR1	Plain	Yes (12/1959)	Yes	11/11/1967
No. 70032	*Tennyson*	12/1952	BR1	Plain	Yes (8/1959)	Yes	30/09/1967
No. 70033	*Charles Dickens*	12/1952	BR1	Plain	Yes (4/1959)	Yes	15/07/1967
No. 70034	*Thomas Hardy*	12/1952	BR1	Plain	Yes (4/1959)	Yes	06/05/1967
No. 70035	*Rudyard Kipling*	12/1952	BR1	Plain	Yes	Yes	30/12/1967
No. 70036	*Boadicea*	12/1952	BR1	Plain	Yes (1959)	Yes	15/10/1966
No. 70037	*Hereward the Wake*	12/1952	BR1	Plain	Yes (10/1960)	Yes	05/11/1966

BR Number	Name	Date Built	Original Tender	Original Coupling Rods	AWS	Speedometer (Smith Stone type)	Withdrawn
No. 70038	*Robin Hood*	1/1953	BR1	Plain	Yes (7/1959)	Yes	12/08/1967
No. 70039	*Sir Christopher Wren*	2/1953	BR1	Plain	Yes (6/1959)	Yes	23/09/1967
No. 70040	*Clive of India*	3/1953	BR1	Plain	Yes (2/1959)	Yes	15/04/1967
No. 70041	*Sir John Moore*	3/1953	BR1	Plain	Yes (7/1941)	Yes	15/04/1967
No. 70042	*Lord Roberts*	4/1953	BR1	Plain	Never Fitted	Never Fitted	15/03/1967
No. 70043	*Lord Kitchener*	6/1953	BR1	Plain	Yes	Yes	07/08/1965
No. 70044	*Earl Haig*	6/1953	BR1	Plain	Yes (2/1961)	Yes (1955)	24/10/1966
No. 70045	*Lord Rowallan*	6/1954	BR1D	Plain	Yes (10/1958)	Fitted from new	30/12/1967
No. 70046	*Anzac*	6/1954	BR1D	Plain	Yes (5/1959)	Fitted from new	08/07/1967
No. 70047	Never named	6/1954	BR1D	Plain	Yes (5/959)	Yes	29/07/1967
No. 70048	*The Territorial Army*	7/1954	BR1D	Plain	Yes (11/1958)	Fitted from new	06/05/1967
No. 70049	*Solway Firth*	7/1954	BR1D	Plain	Yes (3/1959)	Fitted from new	09/12/1967
No. 70050	*Firth of Clyde*	8/1954	BR1D	Plain	Yes	Fitted from new	06/08/1966
No. 70051	*Firth of Forth*	8/1954	BR1D	Plain	Yes (3/1963)	Fitted from new	16/12/1967
No. 70052	*Firth of Tay*	8/1954	BR1D	Plain	Yes (1964)	Fitted from new	01/04/1967
No. 70053	*Moray Firth*	9/1954	BR1D	Plain	Yes	Fitted from new	15/04/1967
No. 70054	*Dornoch Firth*	9/1954	BR1D	Plain	Yes (1962)	Fitted from new	26/11/1966

Above:
No. 70035 *Rudyard Kipling* at Crewe works 7 February, 1965. Note how the horn guides were proud of the mainframe and the footplate support brackets attached to the boiler. The author also visited the works on the same day! (IA/PLS)

Cab Fittings

Driver's side

- Cylinder Oil Indicator
- Steam Chest Pressure Gauge
- Vacuum Gauge
- Whistle Valve Handle
- Gradual Steam Brake Valve
- Driver's Brake Valve, Vacuum Relief Valve & Release Valve
- Regulator
- Small Ejector Steam Valve
- Large Ejector Steam Valve
- Blower Valve
- Reversing Gear
- Cylinder Cock Operating Handle
- Sanding Valve
- Steam Brake Lubricator

Fireman's Side

- Steam Manifold Main Shut-off Valve
- Water Gauges
- Carriage Warming Pressure Gauge
- Carriage Warming Reducing Valve
- Boiler Pressure Gauge
- Firehole Doors
- Exhaust Steam Injector Steam Valve
- Live Steam Injector Feed Water Valve
- Exhaust Steam Injector Feed Water Valve
- Coal Watering Cock
- Tender Sprinkler Valve
- Damper Control
- Live Steam Injector Feed Water Valve
- Rocking Grate Levers

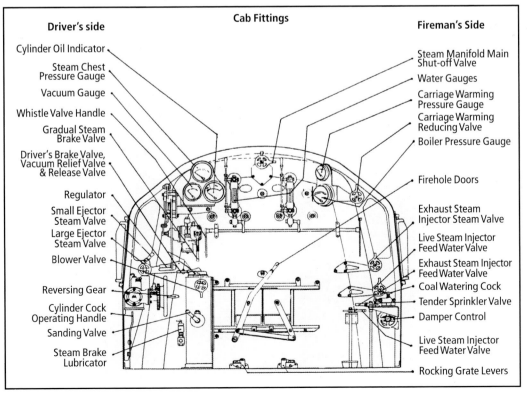

Above:
The firehole door in the open position with the operation lever at left. (DC)

Far left:
The driver's position in the cab of No 70000 *Britannia*. The large wheel at centre controlled the reversing gear. (DC)

MANIFOLD
SHUT OFF
VALVE

OPEN

SHUT

WHISTLE

SMALL EJECTOR
LARGE EJECTOR

BLOWER

SAND
BACK FORE

OIL CANS

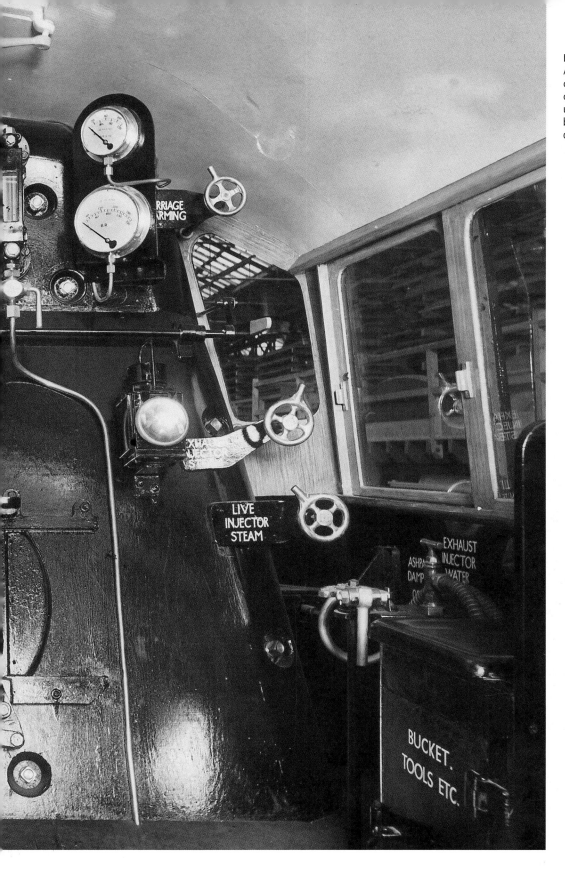

CHAPTER TWO

CONSTRUCTION

As each batch of the class was built, the opportunity
was taken to make design changes from batch to batch
to improve performance and efficiency.

The 'Britannia' class was built in three
batches (the official terminology was Lot
Numbers) and all were built at Crewe works.

Batch 1 being Nos. 70000 to 70024, built
between January and October 1951

Batch 2, Nos. 70025 to 70044, built between
September 1952 and July 1953

Batch 3, Nos. 70045 to 70054, built in 1954.

As each batch was built the opportunity was
taken to make some design changes from batch
to batch as described below. As the class took
three years to complete building this gave
sufficient time for modifications to be sketched
out and implemented. The imperatives to
modify were the same as they have always been,
but there was a greater preparedness to actually
change things for the better.

1. Items that broke, or did not work effectively
included:
a. Wheels moving on the axle
b. Tender to locomotives coupling pin fracturing
c. Movement of slide bars
d. Water carry over into the cylinders.

2. Things that could improve performance,
servicing or crew comfort, this included
changes to the lubrication system (following
excessive wear to piston and valves) and the
fitting of canvas and rubber screens between
the tender and cab.

Some parts of the design did not work
as intended and proved troublesome in service so
the design team then sketched out modifications. In some cases the modification was to
change from say a former LNER design to that
of a former LMS design (as in the change of
the method for fixing the return crank on the
valve gear).

COUPLING RODS

Locomotives from Batch 1 (Nos.70000 to
70024) were built with parallel-fluted coupling
rods whilst locomotives from Batches 2 and 3
(Nos. 70025 to 70054) were built with slightly
tapered plain section rods. This change resulted
from the wheels moving on the axle which
caused severe bending of the coupling rods.
These revised rods were slightly heavier (by 60lb
[27.22kg]) and also resulted in changes to the
balance weights.

Some of the Batch 1 locomotives were
subsequently equipped with replacement plain
rods, but several ended up with a mixture of
plain and fluted rods although with the
exception of No. 70031 *Byron* (which acquired
fluted rear rods in 1957) none of the Batch 2 and
3 locomotives ever carried fluted rods. Examples
of mixed rods (usually plain front and fluted
rear) include No. 70004 *William Shakespeare*,

Above:
No 70028 *Royal Star* in 1956, on the up 'Red Dragon', with original smoke deflectors. (CR/PA)

Left:
No 70037 *Hereward the Wake* at Liverpool Lime Street 'blowing off' before departing with the down 'Norfolkman' in May 1956. (CR/PGL)

Right:
LMS-style four-bolt
fixing for the return
crank. Note also
the solid axle.
The small hole is
a turning centre
for machining the
wheels and tyres.
(IA/JRS)

No. 70005 *John Milton*, No. 70014 *Iron Duke*, No. 70015 *Apollo*, No. 70016 *Ariel*, No. 70019 *Lightning*, No. 70020 *Mercury*, No. 70021 *Morning Star* and No. 70024 *Vulcan*.

Subsequently some of the Batch 1 locomotives were seen with mixed rods had the fluted rods eliminated completely and had plain rods throughout. Examples include No. 70005 John Milton, No. 70007 *Coeur-de-*

Lion, No. 70013 *Oliver Cromwell*, No. 70018 *Flying Dutchman*, No. 70021 *Morning Star* and No. 70025 *Western Star*.

COUPLED WHEELS AXLES

Batch 1 locomotives (Nos. 70000 to 70024) were built with hollow axles (used on a number of LMS classes) as a weight saving exercise but on

Left:
No. 70008 *Black Prince* at Leeds (Holbeck) shed in July 1964. The modified front step is clearly visible. The top lamp bracket has been lowered on the smokebox door and the corresponding bracket on the footplate moved sideways to match the moved bracket. LMS-style smoke deflectors have been fitted (note the 'cups' behind the slots). The 'bash' plate for the AWS equipment is clearly visible. (DC)

the 'Britannia' class this proved to be a mistake as on some locomotives the wheels moved on the axles leading to the class being temporarily withdrawn for modifications. This involved replacing the axle with a solid type although some axles were 'plugged' (as a temporary measure) with an insert in the end of the axle to a depth that corresponded to the thickness of the wheel.

Batch 2 and 3 locomotives were built with solid axles from new and looked the same as the modified locomotives from Batch 1.

RETURN CRANK FIXING

The whole class was built with forked return cranks secured by a clamping bolt as per LNER practice. However from 1956 onwards

Above:
The bracket for the speedometer drive bolted to the crank of the rear driving wheel. (DC)

Right:
The trailing truck fitted with Timken roller bearings. The cover is painted yellow with a horizontal red stripe for identification. Note the live steam injector and also the small air tank which was for the AWS equipment. (DC)

Above:
The balance weights are formed by two plates at the front and back of the wheel attached by countersunk rivets. When the wheels were balanced, molten lead was poured into the pockets created between the spokes and the crescent shaped plates. (DC)

Left:
The trailing truck fitted with roller bearings. The cover plate fitted above the spring and axlebox was an attempt to keep out ash and debris. (DC)

Above:
No. 70004 *William Shakespeare* as built in 1951. There are holes through the axle, LNER-style fixing for the return crank and fluted rods. Note the additional lubricator where the rods meet. This was removed when replacement solid coupling rods were fitted. (IA/CRLC)

Far right:
No. 70027 *Rising Star* at Gloucester shed, fitted with WR-pattern modified smoke deflectors. (IA/JRS)

the return cranks were fixed using the LMS method of four studs set into the crankpin. Most of the class were modified but two locomotives remained unmodified until withdrawal: No. 70004 *William Shakespeare* and No. 70024 *Vulcan*.

DRIVING WHEEL BALANCE WEIGHTS

On the Batch 1 locomotives (Nos. 70000 to 70024) the centre driving wheel balance weight covered the space between seven spokes but with the change to the lighter plain rods on Batch 2 and Batch 3 locomotives the balance weights were changed to cover only the space between six spokes (presumably to compensate for the additional weight of the coupling rods). However this relationship between coupling rods and balance weights was not always maintained. When some of the Batch 1

locomotives were fitted with plain and fluted coupling rods the original balance weights were retained (examples including No. 70004 *William Shakespeare*, No. 70014 *Iron Duke* and No. 70023 *Venus*). Some of the Batch 2 locomotives built with plain rods and the six space balance weights subsequently acquired the Batch 1 seven space balance weights.

TRAILING TRUCK BEARINGS

The class was fitted with BR/Timken-type roller bearing axleboxes to the trailing trucks. However Nos. 70040 to 70049 were built with LMS-pattern plain bearing axleboxes, identified by a different cover. To resolve lubrication problems these plain bearings were fitted with an external oil-feed pipe, fed by a small reservoir just above the axlebox. The external pipe was subsequently removed when a larger rectangular reservoir was incorporated in the top half of the axlebox cover. On one

Above:
The handrails as fitted to the cabs of locomotives with the BR1 and BR1A tenders. The arrangements for those fitted with the BR1D were different , the rear handrail on the cab being deleted and replaced by one on the tender front. (DC)

Above right:
The water space between the inner and outer fireboxes could accumulate sludge and scale. On the 'Britannia' and 'Clan' boiler the access to clean this out was provided as shown. The blanking plate (fitted using a clamp) is removed. (DC)

Left:
The valve gear and motion was a mixture of LMS and LNER practice with the slide bar and crosshead following LNER practice and the wheels being in the LMS style. The front face of the lubricator is now visible; when built the first 25 locomotives had the lubricator covered by the vertical foot plating. The pushrod for the lubricator is in this case angled. When built all locomotives had the pushrod parallel with the rails, but subsequently many were modified as per this photograph. (DC)

Far left:
The BR Standard classes had a steam manifold placed outside the cab (on the boiler top) which supplied steam to the various fittings. This view shows the some of the pipe work associated and clearly shows the operating rods emerging from the cab front. Also visible is the whistle cord which passed through the handrail tubing to reach the whistle. (DC)

Above:
No. 70014 *Iron Duke* at Willesden shed in June 1964 featuring most of the modifications applied to the class. Below the nameplate are four bolts where the 'Golden Arrow' symbol was located on the smoke deflectors. Note the sloping pushrod to the lubricator. (DC)

Right:
No. 70016 *Ariel* at Edinburgh Waverley in September 1961, still showing Western Region origins: WR-style lamp brackets, route availability spot on the cabside, modified smoke deflectors and ejector. The locomotive was now allocated to Carlisle (Canal). (DC)

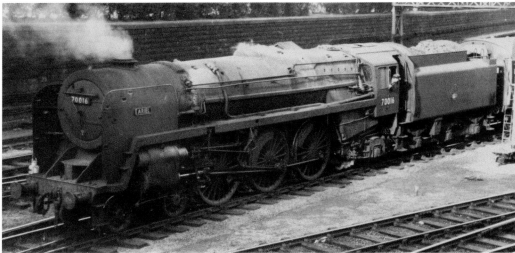

locomotive (No. 70042 *Lord Roberts*) the plain bearings were replaced with a roller bearing set and these were retained until withdrawal.

SMOKE DEFLECTORS

When built, all the deflectors were fitted with a simple handrail parallel to the edge. However following the accident at Milton in 1955 involving a Western Region (WR) allocated locomotive (No. 70026 *Polar Star*) the WR modified its allocation on the basis that the handrail may have contributed to the lack of visibility which was a factor in the accident. The handrail was removed and replaced by recessed handholds in the

deflector. Subsequently other regions also modified the deflectors with handholds but the designs varied and as with all such modifications not all locomotives were so fitted. Some of the WR locomotives having been modified with the Region's type, also subsequently received a modified second type. The types and fitment (by withdrawal) were as follows:

1. Retained original handrails. Nos. 70004, 70014, 70021, 70031, 70032, 70033, 70042, 70043, 70045, 70046, 70047, 70048, 70049, 70050, 70051 and 70052.
2. Western Region type with six rectangular handhold slots. Nos. 70015, 70016, 70018, 70019, 70022, 70023, 70025, 70026 and

70027. These were made of brass and some locomotives ran with these unpainted and polished.

3. London Midland Region type 1. Two circular handholds (with cupped backing plate) plus an additional horizontal handrail level with the top of the footplate on the deflector. Nos. 70000, 70001, 70002, 70003, 70005, 70006, 70007, 70008, 70009, 70010, 70011, 70012, 70013, 70030, 70034, 70035, 70036, 70037, 70038, 70039, 70040, 70041, 70044, 70053 and 70054.

4. London Midland Region type 2. Two circular handholds without a cupped backing plate, with an additional horizontal handrail level with the top of the footplate

on the deflector. Nos. 70017, 70020, 70024, 70028 and 70029.

In addition to these styles of smoke deflectors, the two locomotives temporarily allocated to the Southern Region (No. 70004 *William Shakespeare* and No. 70014 *Iron Duke*) had four holes in each deflector to bolt on the 'Golden Arrow' emblem. When the arrow was not fitted four bolts filled in the holes. Subsequently after moving away from the Southern Region these two locomotives had four bolt heads visible on the deflectors and these were retained until withdrawal. No. 70004 *William Shakespeare* was fitted with a replacement deflector (on the right-hand side) at Darlington works in 1965 following

Above:
No. 70025 *Western
Star* at Crewe.
The battery for
the ATC apparatus is
clearly visible under
the cab. The axles
are now solid, and
the cover on the
lubricator is now
removed. (DC)

accident damage and so lost this feature (but retained this for the left-hand deflector). At the time of this repair all the cast nameplates had been removed but certainly in photographs taken in 1966 and 1967 holes for the nameplate are clearly visible in the replacement deflector and it is assumed that this was done when the replacement was fitted at Darlington works.

EJECTORS

When the Western Region modified the smoke deflectors on the 'Britannia' class, the WR also decided to relocate the brake ejector to a lower position on the boiler. This modification was only carried out on the WR allocated locomotives including: No. 70015 *Apollo*, No. 70016 *Ariel*, No. 70019 *Lightning*, No. 70024 *Vulcan*, No. 70027 *Royal Star*, No. 70028 *Rising Star* and No. 70029 *Shooting Star*.

FRONT VACUUM PIPE

The Batch 1 locomotives (Nos. 70000 to 70024) were built with the vacuum pipe on the front bufferbeam projected above the top of the beam but for the remainder of the class the vacuum pipe only came to the bottom third of the buffer-beam. These 25 locomotives were subsequently modified to match the rest of the class, but again this took some time to complete.

DOME CHANGES

As built the dome on the top of the boiler was very compact but there were problems with water carry over into the cylinders (causing damage to the pistons and piston rods). This problem appeared very quickly and required urgent rectification; the solution was to modify the dome and externally this appears as much larger. Photographic analysis of the locomotives as built indicates that the modified domes were

fitted new from No. 70007 *Coeur-de-Lion*. Further locomotives in the class were built with the revised dome and the earlier locomotives were immediately modified.

LAMP IRONS

On the SR the lamp brackets were modified to allow route orientation head codes. On the WR the lamp brackets were modified to mount the GWR-style lamps.

From 1963 the top lamp bracket was lowered for safety reasons; this required the middle lower lamp bracket to be moved to the right to line up with the relocated top bracket.

SAND BOX LIDS

As built, locomotives Nos. 70000 to 70029 were fitted with two sandboxes with the lids flush to the footplate top, the two sandboxes feeding all three sets of drivers. All the following locomotives (Nos. 70030 to 70054) were fitted with three sandboxes. Those originally fitted with two sandboxes retained them and were not fitted with the additional sandbox (certainly No. 70004 *William Shakespeare*, No. 70014 *Iron Duke*, No. 70015 *Apollo*, No. 70021 *Morning Star*, No. 70024 *Vulcan* and No. 70025 *Western Star* were still fitted with two sandboxes [but with raised lids – see below] into the 1960s).

When built both two and three sandbox lids were flush but subsequently the lids were raised above the foot plating. However not all locomotives in the class were fitted with the raised sandbox lids, certainly the following never appeared to have received these: No. 70000 *Britannia*, No. 70001 *Lord Hurcomb*, No. 70002 *Geoffrey Chaucer*, No. 70003 *John Bunyon*, No. 70005 *John Milton*, No. 70006 *Robert Burns*, No. 70007 *Coeur-de-Lion*, No. 70009 *Alfred the Great*, No. 70010 *Owen Glendower*, No. 70012 *John of Gaunt* and No. 70013 *Oliver Cromwell*.

Above:
No. 70013 *Oliver Cromwell* at Crewe in 1953. The original two steps underneath the smokebox are visible. The vacuum pipe has already been reduced in height. (DC)

35

Above:
No. 70017 *Arrow*
on the Western
Region soon after
completion. The
tall vacuum pipe
remains, but the
lubricator cover has
been removed. The
hollow axles have
also been replaced.
Note the square box
between the front
bogie wheels; this is
the ATC contact
shoe. The sandbox
lids (two) are now
raised, but the
original steps under
the smokebox
remain. (DC)

One of the class, No. 70027 *Royal Star*, appears to have had a unique modification in that it ran with a backing plate around three sides of its two sandbox covers. Presumably this was a Swindon modification, but I have been unable to find any photographic evidence that any other member of the class received these. These were removed by the mid–1960s.

OVAL BUFFERS

No. 70045 *Lord Rowallan* was fitted with oval buffers in 1966; these were retained until withdrawal. It is not known where these buffers came from or why they were fitted.

HINGED FRONT CAB WINDOWS

Following complaints from crews that the front windows became dirty and could not be easily cleaned, from 1957 the following locomotives were modified with opening cab front windows: Nos. 70004, 70014, 70015, 70017, 70031, 70032, 70033, 70042, 70043 and 70044.

COVER PLATE TO LUBRICATOR

As built Batch 1 locomotives (Nos. 7000 to 70024) had the vertical foot plating continuous

along the whole length covering the front face of the mechanical lubricator box. However from 1952 onwards the section covering the front face of the lubricator was removed, and all the class was soon modified. This was presumably to make maintenance easier by improving access to the lubricator.

REGULATOR ROD BRACKET

As built the external regulator rod was only supported at the ends; subsequently steadying brackets, one between the smokebox and the intermediate fulcrum and one on the firebox side, were fitted. However not all the class received both with a number not receiving the one on the firebox side.

LUBRICATOR PUSHROD

As built all the lubricator pushrods were parallel to the coupling rods but subsequently the vertical portion of the mechanism was shortened thus making the pushrod angled. This would increase the rate of oil delivery, but this modification would appear to have been very inconsistent as the original type would be seen subsequently on the same locomotive. In one documented case the same

Above:
Detail of the AWS
equipment 'bash'
plate and contact
shoe on No 70000.
Note the lowered
vacuum pipe. (DC)

locomotive had both types of pushrod, a different one on each side.

FRONT STEP

As originally built there were two steps fixed to the inside of the mainframes below the smokebox door. This was revised with a much larger step with a central support brake which covered the space between the front frames, although No. 70018 *Flying Dutchman* was seen for a short period with a larger step, but without the support bracket. Another locomotive No. 70000 *Britannia*, was seen with a very narrow support bracket fitted.

AIR BRAKES

No. 70043 *Lord Kitchener* and No. 70044 *Earl Haig* were built with air braking equipment in June 1953 which necessitated the fitment of two large air pumps on the front of each locomotive, thus preventing the fitment of smoke deflectors. A number of trials were conducted in 1953-54 with these two locomotives on the benefits of air braking. Once the trials were completed these two locomotives continued in service with the air pumps fitted until these were removed in April

1957 and smoke deflectors fitted. Why it took so long to remove the air brake equipment following the completion of the trials remains a mystery.

SPEEDOMETERS

The last batch of 'Britannia' class locomotives built (Nos. 70045 to 70054) were fitted from new with the Smith Stone-type speedometer which had became the standard fitment to BR steam locomotives across all regions. Following this, many of the class built without it, received this fitment but as with many other classes not all locomotives received the equipment before withdrawal. Known examples not receiving the speedometer by withdrawal include No. 70023 *Venus*, No. 70024 *Vulcan*, No. 70027 *Royal Star* and No. 70028 *Rising Star*.

ATC AND AWS EQUIPMENT

When built, the class was not fitted with AWS but those allocated to the Western Region were fitted with Automatic Train Control (ATC).

The ATC equipment could be identified by the following:

Above:
No. 70044 *Earl Haig* at Bangor in July 1963, coupled to BR1 tender. Note the cab has two handrails. Plain bearings are fitted on the trailing truck. There is a small air tank under the cab as part of the AWS installation. The support bracket for the regulator rod is mounted on the side of the firebox. (IA)

1. Battery box under the cab (left-hand side only).
2. Pipe (conduit) along the whole length of the foot plate (sometimes passing under the lubricator)
3. No 'bash' plate under the front buffer beam
4. Box-like contact shoe bolted to the front of the bogie.

Locomotives known to have been fitted with ATC include No. 70018 *Flying Dutchman*, No. 70019 *Lightning*, No. 70021 *Morning Star*, No. 70022 *Tornado*, No. 70023 *Venus*, No. 70025 *Western Star*, No. 70026 *Polar Star* and No. 70027 *Royal Star*.

Between 1957 and 1963 the BR standard Automatic Warning System (AWS) was fitted, and was evident by the following:

1. Contact shoe attached to the front of the bogie; this was circular and less conspicuous than the ATC type.
2. 'Bash' plate fitted to prevent the front coupling swinging back and damaging the contact shoe.
3. Pipe clipped to the left-hand platform and running along the platform to the air tank under the cab.

4. Battery box located on the footplate on the right-hand side of the locomotive.
5. Small circular cylinder under the bottom of the cab on the left-hand (driver's) side.

The majority of the class were eventually fitted with AWS but as with speedometer fitment not all received the equipment. Examples which were never fitted include No. 70004 *William Shakespeare*, No. 70015 *Apollo*, No. 70016 *Ariel*, No. 70017 *Arrow*, No. 70023 *Venus*, No. 70024 *Vulcan*, No. 70026 *Polar Star*, No. 70027 *Royal Star* and No. 70028 *Rising Star*.

A number of locomotives were fitted with AWS with battery box and 'bash' plate but the small air tank under the cab and its associated pipework is not visible, presumably being located in a position out of view. Examples include No. 70046 *Anzac*, No. 70048 *The Territorial Army 1908-1958* and No. 70051 *Firth of Forth*. Certainly No. 70048 *The Territorial Army 1908-1958* had an air tank mounted on the right-hand footplate as a replacement but the other two did not. The reason for this modification is not known to the author.

No. 70045 *Lord Rowallan* showing why when fitted to a BR1D tender the second vertical cab handrail had to be removed as a handrail was already fitted to the tender. Note the plain axlebox, with modified cover and a large oil reservoir, also the bracket fitted on the cabside for drivers name. (IA/PG)

The usual fitment for AWS had the battery box located on the right-hand footplate but at least three locomotives (No. 70014 *Iron Duke*, No. 70025 *Western Star* and No. 70048 *The Territorial Army 1908-1958*) also had a long air tank fitted on the top of the footplate in front of the battery box on the right-hand footplate.

TENDERS

The tenders for the 'Britannias' were of a new design and were intended to be self trimming but in this respect the design was not completely successful. The three tender types fitted to the class were as follows:

BR1. These were fitted to the majority of the class and had 7 tons (7,112.3kg) coal capacity with 4,250 gallons (19,110 litres) water capacity. In theory the tenders had a water capacity of 5000 gallons (22,750 litres) but the actual capacity was limited by the water pick up arrangements. These were also fitted to the 10 'Clan' class and to 50 of the BR 4-6-0 Standard Class 5.

BR 1A. These were superficially identical to the BR1 type and were fitted to Nos. 70025 to 70029 from new with capacity for 5000 gallons (22,750 litres) water and 7 tons (7,112.3kg) coal, and were built because of insufficient water capacity. Internal plates were modified to allow the extra 750 gallons (3,412.5 litres) water capacity, and were recognizable from the BR1 tenders by the larger (taller) dome above the water pick up apparatus.

BR1D. These were fitted from new on Nos. 70045 to 70054 and had a 9 tons (9,144.4kg) coal capacity, carried 4,750 gallons (21,612.5 litres) water and were fitted with a coal pusher. These tenders would allow longer runs without refuelling such as the Holyhead to Euston service and some Glasgow to Manchester and Glasgow to Liverpool services. The original BR1 tenders compared unfavourably with tenders fitted to such classes as the ex-LMS re-built Scots which had a 9 tons (9,144.4kg) coal capacity. When the 'Britannia' class (fitted with the BR1 tenders) was first used on the Holyhead to Euston trains it was marginal on fuel and the locomotives concerned were soon moved away. It was only with the introduction of the BR1D tenders that

'Britannias' were re-allocated to Holyhead. The new BR1D tenders were very similar externally to tenders fitted to the last of the ex-LMS 'Duchess' class of 4-6-2 (officially 'Princess Coronation' class) and as with the later 'Duchesses' tenders were fitted with a steam-powered coal pusher to assist the fireman. These tenders remained with the last five locomotives until withdrawal but as noted elsewhere when three of the class were withdrawn the tenders were re-used fitted to No. 70012 *John of Gaunt*, No. 70014 *Iron Duke* and No. 70034 *Thomas Hardy*. It is not known if the steam connections to power the coal pushers were also installed but it is unlikely.

As the vertical cab handrails were different for locomotives originally fitted with the BR1D tender (the handrail being on the tender), locomotives formerly fitted with BR1 tenders would need modifications to accommodate the BR1D tender. Certainly No. 70014 *Iron Duke* and No. 70034 *Thomas Hardy* both retained the second cab handrail but had the tender handrail removed to allow the BR1D tender to be fitted.

TENDER FOOTSTEP

As built, the Batch 1 locomotives (Nos. 70000 to 70024) were fitted with BR1 tenders and did not have the step adjacent to the water-filler hole on each side of the tender but this was subsequently added to Batch 2 locomotives which had the step fitted from new and the Batch 1 locomotives were modified.

TENDER EXCHANGES

Tender exchanges normally took place at works and the 'Britannia' class was no exception; those that exchanged tenders usually kept the same type as originally fitted. However the swapping of tenders at sheds was a regular feature in the mid-1960s as shed foremen kept their fleets operational by cannibalising spares from withdrawn loco-motives and three of the class originally fitted with BR1 tenders acquired BR1D tenders as follows:

No. 70014 *Iron Duke*. This was photo-graphed with a BR1D tender from January 1967 following a visit to Crewe works, but it is not clear if the locomotive entered the works

Above:
No. 70026 *Polar Star* at Cardiff (Canton) depot. The two sandbox lids are clearly visible. A post 1957 BR totem is on the side of the tender. Plain rods are fitted as are WR-pattern replacement smoke deflectors. (IA/GFH)

with this substitute tender (probably being fitted at Carlisle shed) or whether it was fitted at Crewe. It was photographed in October 1966 at Carlisle (Kingmoor) still with a BR1 tender. The most likely answer is that the tender was fitted immediately before entering Crewe as two locomotives with BR1D tenders (No. 70050 *Firth of Clyde* withdrawn in August 1966 and No. 70054 *Dornoch Firth* withdrawn in November 1966) were stored at Carlisle (Kingmoor) during November and December 1966 (the locomotives were not scrapped at Crewe) so that it is almost certain that one of these withdrawn locomotives had its tender fitted to No. 70014 *Iron Duke*.

No. 70034 *Thomas Hardy*, was also fitted with a BR1D tender some time in late 1966 or early 1967. The acquired tender was numbered 985 and would have come, like the tender for No. 70014 *Iron Duke*, from either No. 70050 *Firth of Clyde* or No. 70054 *Dornoch Firth*. As No. 70054 was known to have been coupled to tender No. 985 the chances are that the tender came from that locomotive which was stored at Carlisle from withdrawal at the end of November 1966 until taken away for scrap in May 1967. Certainly No. 70034 *Thomas Hardy* was seen with the 'new' tender in March 1967.

No. 70012 *John of Gaunt* acquired a BR1D tender very late in service, getting this tender

in October 1967, before being withdrawn in December 1967. The list of potential candidates for supplying the tender is long. By October 1967 the following locomotives fitted with BR1D tenders were withdrawn and stored at Carlisle (Kingmoor): No. 70046 *Anzac*, No. 70047 (unnamed), No. 70048 *The Territorial Army*, No. 70052 *Firth of Tay* and No. 70053 *Moray Firth*, providing plenty of choice to the shed foreman looking for a replacement tender. Interestingly enough there were a number of other 'Britannias' with BR1 and BR1A tenders also withdrawn and stored at Kingmoor at the same time. No. 70012 *John of Gaunt* required a new tender but the choice of substitute was a BR1D, not a straight swap for a BR1 or BR1A; the reason for this is unknown.

As has been mentioned earlier the locomotives retained the original cab handrails but the tender handrails were modified to allow running behind these locomotives.

TENDER & CAB SIDE SCREENS

Following complaints, by crews, of draughty cabs from 1952 onwards a canvas and rubber screen was fitted between the cab and tender in an attempt to improve the situation but this was not completely successful.

Left:
The front of the BR1 and BR1A tender as fitted to most of the 'Britannia' class. No fall plate is provided as the extended cab floor would ensure a single platform for the crew, as the coal access hole would sit over the cab floor. The water gauge can be seen on the right below the window. (DC)

No. 70035 *Rudyard Kipling* passes Carlisle (Kingmoor) in early 1964 on a freight train. This perfectly illustrates the mixed-traffic capacity of the 'Britannia' class. The second to sixth vehicles are Palvans, BR's first attempt at specialised vehicles designed for carrying pallets. (DC)

CHAPTER THREE

LIVERIES & NAMES

When built the 'Britannias' were painted in lined–out
BR Dark Green with brass nameplates, but ended their days
in drab unlined 'economy' green with painted names.

When first built No. 70000 *Britannia* ran trials in unlined black, before being repainted in the standard BR Dark Green livery. However it ran for a few days in lined green before receiving its nameplate.

LIVERIES

Livery for the 'Britannia' class was as follows: The locomotive (except for the black as described below) was painted in BR Green. The boiler bands (except those on the firebox) were lined out in orange and black. The vertical surface of the footplate had a single orange line a little way in from the edge with rounded curves at each end effectively forming a very elongated rectangle. The tender top was also painted green.

The smokebox and cab roof were painted black, and the firebox cladding below the footplate was also black but Doncaster appears to have painted its 'Britannias' with green firebox cladding (No. 70038 *Robin Hood* was seen at Doncaster works in 1959). When AWS was fitted the battery box was usually painted black. The cab doors were certainly unlined black when the green livery was applied, but were painted green when lined out.

Early Totem, the original totem painted on the tender was the large type.

Later Totem, the first 'Britannia' to receive the new totem was No. 70016 *Ariel* in June

1956, but No. 70004 *William Shakespeare* was observed with the early totem as late as 1960. A locomotive was not necessarily given a full repaint when visiting main works for attention so hence the early totem lasted until 1960. Again the usual size was the large type, however No. 70003 *John Byron* was seen in 1965 with the small totem when painted in unlined green.

Power Classification. When painted in both lined and unlined green a simple numeral 7 was painted just above the locomotive number. As the class was classified 7MT (signifying Mixed Traffic) it is surprising that this was not painted on the cab side. However as always there were a number of exceptions, No. 70042 *Lord Roberts* was seen in 1962 with 7P on the cab side. In 1965 No. 70052 *Firth of Tay* was seen in unlined green also with 7P on the cab side.

Cylinder Lining. The cylinders were painted black and were originally lined out with two vertical red lines at each end. However as the locomotives went through works for maintenance many were repainted with the lining omitted. This variability in lining also occurred with other ex-LMS classes. Many had the cylinders lined out but Crewe especially appears to have been inconsistent in using this lining. Those observed with lining (dates given) are as follows: No. 70010 (1960s), No. 70018 (1963), No. 70019 (1957), No. 70021 (1964, but

Above:
No. 70052 *Firth of Tay* at Nottingham on a rail tour in April 1965. No. 70052 is in plain green, but still with a name-plate and 7P on the cabside. (CR)

Left:
No. 70052 *Firth of Tay* at Preston fitted with a BR1D coal-pusher tender. The style of lining for this type of tender is clearly visible. (CR)

not in 1962), No. 70022 (1960), No. 70028 (1957), No. 70046 (1959), No. 70048 (1963) and No. 70050 (1963 at Crewe works). Certainly 'Britannias' overhauled at Doncaster did not appear to have lined out cylinders, No. 70023 *Venus* from Cardiff (Canton) was seen ex-works without lining in 1961. There does not appear to have been any consistency in the application of this lining.

BR Unlined Green. An instruction was sent out in December 1963 to stop the lining-out of black painted locomotives and it is also assumed that green locomotives were not to be lined from this time. It is known that some works took a little time to conform to this directive (particularly St. Rollox in Scotland) and certainly 'Black 5s' were still being lined-out in early 1964 when out-shopped from this works.

The majority of locomotives at the beginning of 1964 were still in lined green livery and with original nameplates. The nameplates were later removed during 1965.

The first sighting I have of the 'economy' green livery was No. 70024 *Vulcan* in July 1964 complete with nameplates, unusual with un-lined green. The green also appeared to be a different shade (darker) than that previously used, almost similar to that of army

'khaki'. In the author's opinion the colour was very drab. Unfortunately 'Britannia' locomotives were very often so dirty that it was difficult to see the true colour. When No. 70013 *Oliver Cromwell* received a final overhaul in February 1967 it was painted in fully lined livery. No. 70013 was the last BR steam locomotive to receive an overhaul before the complete demise of steam.

Also because the new 'economy' green colour was just painted over the original lined green it was a fairly simple exercise to rub this off revealing the lining underneath. No. 70038 *Robin Hood* was observed on an enthusiasts' special with full lining on the cab side but with an unlined tender. No. 70004 *William Shakespeare* was also observed in 1966 in a 'hybrid' livery when also cleaned for an enthusiasts' special.

It is difficult to clearly identify which member of the class was the last to have retained the original lined livery (excepting No. 70013 *Oliver Cromwell*) but certainly a number were painted in fully lined livery in 1965 after removal of nameplates, No. 70050 *Firth of Clyde* was observed in July 1965. However by this date the majority would have carried the 'economy' green livery.

Tender Lining (variations). The BR1D tenders were finished with the lining following the shape of the tender. However in the early 1960s on No. 70050 *Firth of Clyde* and No. 70053 *Moray Firth* the tender was lined out as a rectangle similar to the green painted Standard Class 5. On the basis that both these locomotives were overhauled at Crewe it is not clear why this had been carried out as other BR1D tenders received the curved lining.

Cab roof (which parts painted black and which parts green). There appears to have been some variation in the painting of the cab roof. On some the whole roof is painted black, but some had the bottom third section of the roof painted green (certainly No. 70050 *Firth of Clyde* seen ex-works in 1962 shows this). The major problem in analysing photographs for this variation is that the locomotives were not very clean making it difficult to be exactly sure what colour the roof is painted.

'Route Availability' Indicator. On the Western Region all locomotives carried a coloured 'spot' below the locomotive number on the cab side (approx 2in [5cm] in diameter) indicating what routes the locomotives were allowed to work; on the 'Britannia' class this was red. When the locomotives were removed from

the Western Region these route indicators were left on but would disappear at the next repaint.

Overhead Warning Indicators. From April 1960, following Continental practice, BR started to fit white enamel plates painted with the symbolic warning sign of forked lightning (in red) to strategic positions on the boiler cladding to alert staff to the possibility of contact with overhead power wires. As the use of overhead wires for electrification extended there were a number of accidents where steam locomotive crew member came into contact with the wires when either trimming coal, filling the tender with water or fitting lamps. The position of these overhead warning flashes varied from locomotive to locomotive, but the normal placing was as follows:

1. On the smoke deflectors near the bottom handrail.
2. Rear of the tender.
3. On the firebox sides.
4. On the boiler cladding.

Axlebox Covers. When built the tender axlebox covers and also bearing covers on the trailing truck were painted black. However when roller bearing axleboxes were fitted the lubrication changed from oil to grease and this was indicated to maintenance staff by

Above:
No. 70053 *Moray Firth* at Crewe in August 1962. This shows the alternative lining style on BR1D tenders also observed on No. 70050 *Firth of Clyde*. This lining was similar to that applied to the green liveried Standard Class 5s fitted with similar tenders (but without the coal pusher). No. 70053 is fitted, with LMS-style smoke deflectors, AWS and speedometer. (DC)

painting the axlebox covers yellow and a horizontal red stripe.

Buffer Beam Lettering. In 1957, two 'Britannia' locomotives on the Eastern Region were observed with 'BR 7' stencilled on the buffer beam.

NAMEPLATES

There had been much debate about the name to be bestowed on the first locomotive in the class and 'Great Briton' was the leading candidate but Bishop Eric Treacy (a well-known railway

photographer) suggested 'Britannia' and this was accepted. The names selected for the class were a strange mixture with both genders being represented. Initially these were of distinguished Britons (except *Lord Hurcomb* who was the head of the British Transport Commission), but the batch intended for the Western Region used names that had been used on earlier GWR locomotives, then returned to the theme of distinguished Britons (up to No. 70045). Ideas for names for No. 70046, No. 70047 and No. 70048 appear to have caused much debate as these locomotives ran for a number of years

Locomotives that originally ran without names

Number	Date Built	Date Named	Name	Original Name Proposal	Comment
No. 70000	5 January 1951	20 January 1951	*Britannia*		Ran in green livery without nameplates for a few days
No. 70001	14 February 1951	6 March 1951	*Lord Hurcomb*		
No. 70032	10 December 1952	17 March 1953	*Tennyson*		
No. 70043	June 1953	May 1957	*Lord Kitchener*		Nameplate affixed when fitted with deflectors
No. 70044	June 1953	March 1957	*Earl Haig*		Nameplate affixed when fitted with deflectors
No. 70045	June 1954	July 1957	*Lord Rowallan*	Midland	
No. 70046	June 1954	September 1959	*Anzac*	London & North Western	
No. 70047	June 1954	Never named		Lancashire & Yorkshire	
No. 70048	July 1954	July 1958	*The Territorial Army 1908-1958*	Furness	Cast aluminium plate
No. 70049	July 1954	28 May 1960	*Solway Firth*		

without names. A number of alternative names including those of old railway companies were at one time proposed. The last locomotives from No. 70049 *Solway Firth* onwards received Scottish-based names.

All the plates were cast in brass except for No. 70048 *The Territorial Army 1908-1958* which was aluminium, presumably to save weight (as it was the largest plate fitted to a 'Britannia'). Some of the plates also had thicker backing at the top so that effectively the plate would be slightly inclined against the smoke deflectors.

Most of the locomotives were named before entering service but a small number ran for some time without nameplates as indicated on page 50.

Patterns for three other names were found in Crewe works but were never cast or used. These names were Sir John Aspinall, Samuel Johnson and John Ramsbottom. Presumably these were a set of alternative names for No. 70045, No. 70046 and No. 70047.

The plates had one line of lettering with the exception of No. 70048 *Territorial Army 1908-1958* where the name had to run to two lines.

The background colour to the nameplates was usually black certainly at the time of entering traffic but a small number are known to have been painted red at the time of the naming ceremony (No. 70045 *Lord Rowallan* and No. 70048 *The Territorial Army 1908-1958*); others subsequently acquired a red background (see list below).

The following locomotives were seen with a red background to the brass nameplate:

No. 70000 *Britannia* (This appears to have been red through most but not all of service)
No. 70004 *William Shakespeare* (1951)
No. 70005 *John Milton*
No. 70009 *Alfred the Great* (1951)
No. 70014 *Iron Duke* (pre-1957)
No. 70015 *Apollo*
No. 70017 *Arrow*
No. 70018 *Flying Dutchman*
No. 70037 *Hereward the Wake* (seen in black after 1957)
No. 70045 *Lord Rowallan*
No. 70052 *Firth of Tay* (when painted in unlined green)

Blue Background Nameplates. It was common practice for Scottish sheds to paint the background to name and smokebox number plates in pale blue. At least one 'Britannia' appears to have been painted with this colour background to the nameplate, No. 70049 *Solway Firth* (1965).

In early 1964 locomotive No. 70002 *Geoffrey Chaucer* was involved in an accident which resulted in a very bent nameplate on the right-hand side smoke deflectors. It is not known if a new nameplate was provided or if the original was straightened.

Painted Names & Unofficial Plates

Following the removal of the brass nameplates during 1965, a number of the locomotives received painted names during the period 1966/67. These names were not generally applied by railway staff but by a group of dedicated enthusiasts. Many of the names were applied at Lostock Hall shed (Preston) where a 'Britannia' was diagrammed to work a Blackpool to Euston train as far as Crewe. Some 16 'Britannias' were treated in this way at Lostock Hall. With these painted names the opportunity was taken to make some small

adjustments to the name so No. 70031 *Byron* with a painted name became No. 70031 *Lord Byron*. Similarly No. 70010 *Owen Glendower* had two versions of the name, one side being in Welsh *'Owain Glendwr'*.

Some locomotives also ran with replacement plates manufactured in wood at this time (including No. 70032 *Lord Tennyson*).

The list of known painted names is as follows:
No. 70010 *Owen Glendower/ Owain Glendwr* (blue background)
No. 70011 *Hotspur*
No. 70013 *Oliver Cromwell*
No. 70014 *Iron Duke* (with red background).
No. 70015 *Apollo*
No. 70018 *Flying Dutchman*
No. 70025 *Western Star*
No. 70026 *Polar Star*
No. 70031 *Lord Byron/Byron*
No. 70032 *Lord Tennyson* (seen with a wooden nameplate at one point)

No. 70038 *Robin Hood*
No. 70040 *Clive of India* (with blue background).
No. 70045 *Lord Rowallan*

Smokebox Number Plates (Wood). Following the removal of the nameplates in 1965 a number of smokebox number plates were removed by shed staff (or stolen) and in some cases were replaced by wooden plates with hand-painted lettering. Generally speaking these were executed to a good standard and the following locomotives were observed; No. 70004 *William Shakespeare*, No. 70015 *Apollo*, No. 70016 *Ariel*, No. 70019 *Lightning*, No. 70023 *Venus*, No. 70035 *Rudyard Kipling*, No. 70049 *Solway Forth*.

A number of 'Britannias' were also observed without a smokebox number plate at all in 1966/67 including No. 70011 *Hotspur* and No. 70018 *Flying Dutchman*.

PLAQUES & EMBELLISHMENTS

The two 'Britannia' locomotives allocated to the Southern region, No. 70004 *William Shakespeare* and No. 70014 *Iron Duke*, had the smoke deflectors modified to allow the large 'Golden Arrow' symbols to be fitted when working that service. The bolt heads filling the holes remained with the locomotives until withdrawal. When running this service two flags (the Tricolour and Union Jack) were fitted with holders mounted on the top of the buffer beam.

Red Painted Smokebox Door Plate. Some locomotive classes had examples where a single locomotive acquired a red background to the smokebox door plate. In the 'Britannia' class this was No. 70014 *Iron Duke* in 1967.

Above:
The nameplate of No. 70015 *Apollo* fitted to the replacement WR-style smoke deflectors. The plate appears to be a replica of the original, but has four bolts visible. (DC)

Right:
No. 70004 *William Shakespeare* at Eastleigh in the 1950s. The locomotive has fluted rods, holes in axles and original LNER-style crank fixing. Note the fire box cladding below the footplate in black. (CR)

Below:
No. 70038 *Robin Hood* at Doncaster, August 1959. The locomotive is fitted with plain rods and LMS-style smoke deflectors. Note the very slanted rod to the lubricators. (CR)

Below:
No. 70054 *Dornoch
Firth* about to depart
Crewe for Euston,
September 1963.
(CR/DCT)

Above:
No. 70044 at Rugby in 1957, having come off a train with a hot box. Westinghouse air pumps and tanks are still fitted. Note the modified front step and lowered vacuum pipe. (IAAWF)

Right:
No. 70048 *The Territorial Army 1908-1958* at Carlisle (Upperby) shed as a standby locomotive. An additional air tank is mounted on the footplate for the AWS. Note the lowered lamp bracket and original smoke deflectors. (IA)

No. 70014 *Iron Duke* at Manchester in as delivered condition. There are holes in the axle, fluted rods and the LNER-style fixing for the return crank. A cover plate is fitted over the lubricator on footplate edge. The sandbox lids are not raised. (IA/RA)

Below:
No. 70029 *Shooting Star* on the up 'Red Dragon' service at Sonning Cutting, April 1960. (CR/PH)

Above:
No. 70028 *Royal Star* at Potters Bar, June 1963. Note the WR-style route availability 'spot' on the cabside. No. 70028 was never fitted with AWS. The locomotive is hauling LNER Thompson coaching stock. (CR/MS)

Left:
No. 70041 *Sir John Moor* at Carlisle (Kingmoor) in May 1965. The locomotive is painted in plain green. (DC)

No. 70026 *Polar Star* at Edge Hill (Liverpool) with No. 70015 *Apollo* at right. Both locomotives are fitted with WR-style smoke deflectors. (IA/GH)

CHAPTER FOUR

IN SERVICE

'Britannias' were at one time or another based on
every region of British Railways and worked every type
of train from unfitted mineral to express passenger.

The 'Britannia' class at one time or another was based on every region of British Railways and was seen at most cities within England, Scotland and Wales. The class did however receive a mixed reception from drivers ranging from 'worship' by the Great Eastern (GE) crews to total contempt from the Western Region (with the notable exception of Cardiff [Canton]). This was generally due to the 'Britannias' not being like the locomotives they were used to, and drivers were pretty conservative creatures and drove the 'Britannias' in the same way they would say a 'Castle' or rebuilt 'Scot'. This even applied on the London Midland Region where 'Britannias' running out of Holyhead to Euston and Manchester consistently lost time. This was due to driving technique, the rebuilt 'Scots' and 'Patriots' were driven on a partial regulator whilst the 'Britannias' responded best on a full throttle and driving on the cut off.

The 'Britannia' class was used indiscriminately as a Class 7 so crews would only drive a 'Britannia' at irregular intervals. So, with the exception of the Great Eastern section which did not have a comparable locomotive, crews did not become particularly practised at driving the class. The 'Britannia' was generally reliable once the initial teething troubles (such as the wheels moving on the axles and the lubrication system were modified). Many crews were happy to drive them but they were not loved in the same way as a 'Castle' or a 'Duchess', but the 'Britannia' class was more popular with the maintenance staff and when intensively diagrammed (as they were on the Great Eastern section) were capable of exceptional mileages, some of the GE examples clocking up 100,000 miles (160,930km) per year. In early service they were completing four return trips to London from Norwich in a day.

ROUTES

Initial allocations were made to the Great Eastern section where the class revolutionised the express passenger trains from London to Ipswich and Norwich. Subsequent allocations went to the Western Region, being based at London (Old Oak Common), Cardiff (Canton) and Newton Abbot. 'Britannias' were therefore seen on the whole network of ex-GWR main lines. Only in later service at Cardiff were they used on the route from Shrewsbury through Hereford to Cardiff and Bristol.

Seven locomotives (No. 70017 *Arrow*, No. 70023 *Venus*, No. 70024 *Vulcan*, No. 70028 *Royal Star*, No. 70029 *Shooting Star*, No. 70030 *William Wordsworth* and No. 70034 *Thomas Hardy*) were loaned to the Southern Region in May 1953 to replace the temporarily withdrawn 'Merchant Navy' class locomotives. Allocations were as

Above:
No. 70050 *Firth of Clyde*, September 1963. The locomotive is fitted with a speedometer and AWS. The original style smoke deflectors are retained. (CR/SW)

Left:
No. 70020 *Mercury* is serviced at West Hartlepool after arriving with a special train, 13 March 1965. Note the LMS-style smoke deflectors (without backing cups to the hand holes) and the lowered lamp bracket. AWS equipment is not fitted. (IA/ISC)

Above:
No. 70052 *Firth of Tay* at Crewe works. Note the locomotive number stencilled all over the boiler cladding. The locomotive is fitted with AWS, speedometer and the lowered smokebox lamp bracket. (DC)

follows: Exmouth Junction (No. 70024 *Vulcan*, No. 70028 *Royal Star*, No. 70029 *Shooting Star*), Dover (No. 70030 *William Wordsworth*), Salisbury (No. 70017 *Arrow*, No. 70023 *Venus*) and Stewarts Lane (No. 70034 *Thomas Hardy*). The 'Britannias' shared duties with other loaned locomotives including ex-LNER 'V2s' and ex-LMS 'Black 5s'.

When first built a number of 'Britannias' were allocated to Manchester for Midland services through the Peak district, Yorkshire to St. Pancras, but the tight curves on the line proved damaging to frames and bogies amounting to a significant number of locomotives standing idle with additional repairs on shed. This resulted in the 'Britannias' being replaced for the service by rebuilt 'Scots'.

When the Eastern Region's 'Britannia' allocation was moved from Stratford and Norwich to March shed, Cambridgeshire, the locomotives reverted to mainly freight workings but were also used on the Sheffield boat train service which was a March diagram. When new the BR1D tendered locomotives went to Polmadie (Glasgow) to run Glasgow to Manchester services and to Holyhead for the Euston service. Both of these services required 9 ton (9,144.4kg) coal capacity.

Some of the Eastern Region allocations were moved to Immingham (near Grimsby) in 1961 where they were used on accelerated passenger services between Cleethorpes and Grimsby to London (Kings Cross), also the heavy and fast fish trains from Grimsby until 1963 when they were re-allocated.

The 'Britannias' were common visitors up the East Coast main line as far as York but were infrequent visitors north of York through Newcastle to Edinburgh. When the locomotives were concentrated at Carlisle they became more frequent visitors in the Newcastle area.

Before being concentrated at Crewe and Carlisle in 1965 a number were allocated to Nottingham (Annersley) and to Banbury for Great Central services for a short period.

An unusual allocation occurred in the summer of 1965 when three 'Britannias' (Nos. 70045, 70047 and 70053) were allocated to the ex-GWR Wolverhampton (Oxley) shed specifically for working Wolverhampton to Kingswear, Devon, via Bristol and return holiday service. When virtually the whole class was allocated to Carlisle, 'Britannias' would be 'borrowed' by other sheds for summer Saturday traffic for services such as Leeds to Llandudno, North Wales and return.

By 1966 the small allocation not at Carlisle (Kingmoor) were allocated at Stockport (No. 70004 *William Shakespeare*, No. 70015 *Apollo*, No. 70021 *Morning Star*, No. 70026 *Polar Star*, No. 70044 *Earl Haig*) for working heavy parcels trains from Manchester usually to Leeds (including the famous 'Red Bank' parcel trains) which was very often double headed due to the heavy loading on this service and gradients on the route.

With the closure of Carlisle shed in December 1967 (although one locomotive carried out its final working from Carlisle on 2 January 1968) the last survivor, No. 70013 *Oliver Cromwell*, was re-allocated to Carnforth and used on a mixture of service trains and enthusiast specials. This was the locomotive seen by the author at rest on Liverpool (Edge Hill) shed, Easter 1968. It was kept in clean condition.

Above:
No. 70045 *Lord Rowallan* and No. 70031 *Byron* on a southbound parcels train out of Wigan, 23 June 1967. (IA/VB)

Allocations

1954	January 1957	January 1960	January 1963	1965	January 1967
30A Stratford	12 at 30A Stratford	2 at 31B March	13 at 5A Crewe (North)	12 at 5B Crewe (South)	
32A Norwich	2 at 73A Stewarts Lane	19 at 32A Norwich	8 at 1A London (Willesden)	5 at 5A Crewe (North)	
31A Ipswich	11 at 32A Norwich	1 at 32B Ipswich	8 at 12A Carlisle (Kingmoor)	18 at 12A Carlisle (Kingmoor)	29 at 12A Carlisle (Kingmoor)
	15 at 86C Cardiff (Canton)	3 at 1A London (Willesden)	1 at 12C Carlisle (Canal)	10 at 12B Carlisle (Upperby)	
	5 at 9A Manchester	5 at 26A Manchester (Longsight)	4 at 6J Holyhead (Newton Heath)	2 at 9B Manchester (Stockport)	4 at 9B Manchester (Stockport)
	5 at 6J Holyhead	12 at 86C Cardiff (Canton)	1 at 6G Llandudno Junction	4 at 9D Manchester (Trafford Park)	
	5 at 66A Glasgow (Polmadie)	4 at 9E Manchester (Trafford Park)	5 at 21D Birmingham (Aston)	2 at 6J Holyhead	
	2 at Manchester (Longsight)	2 at 2B Wolverhampton (Oxley)			
	4 at 55A Leeds (Holbeck)	1 at 31B March			
	1 at 5A Crewe (North)	4 at 40 Birmingham			
	3 at 66A Glasgow (Polmadie)				

Above:
No. 70020 *Mercury* on rail tour duty at Clapham in March 1964. The locomotive is fitted with fluted rear connecting rods and LMS-style smoke deflectors. No. 70020 was never fitted with a speedometer and does not have AWS. (CR/ RD)

Right:
No. 70032 *Lord Tennyson* at Lostock Hall in 1966. Replacement wooden nameplates are fitted to original smoke deflectors (CR/ MC)

Above:
No. 70051 *Firth of Forth* at Willesden. Original type smoke deflectors are fitted. The locomotives also has AWS equipment and a speedometer. (CR/ MS)

Left:
No. 70006 *Lord Roberts* hauling a freight train at Dent on the Settle-Carlisle line in 1964. (CR/DJM)

Left:
No. 70006 *Robert Burns* on York MPD. Note the AWS conduit clipped to the underside of the footplate, the cable from the speedometer clipped below. The AWS air tank is below the cab. Plain rods are fitted, as are LMS-style smoke deflectors. (IA)

No. 70045 before being named *Lord Rowallan* at Bangor, North Wales, 5 June 1956. The locomotive is fitted with the original type smoke deflectors. A speedometer is fitted. (CR/JM)

REPAIR LOCATIONS

The main works for heavy repairs to the class were Crewe, Swindon and Doncaster.

Logically, the Western Region allocated locomotives should have had major overhauls at Swindon but this was not always the case as in May 1961 No. 70023 *Venus* and No. 70027 *Royal Star* were moved from Cardiff (Canton) to Doncaster for overhaul, travelling via Crewe, Stockport and Wakefield.

Following the closure of Doncaster in November 1963 no 'Britannias' remained on the Western Region from 1963 and from 1964 Crewe took on sole responsibility for major overhauls.

During a 12-month period in 1964, 29 locomotives of the class were observed in Crewe works for repair, most of which involved stays of two months indicating a major overhaul.

The 'Britannias' continued to receive major overhauls at Crewe throughout 1966 and 1967 ending in February 1967 when No. 70013 *Oliver Cromwell* was overhauled. When the author visited Crewe in February 1965 there were six 'Britannias' in works receiving repairs. Unfortunately the Engine History cards were not always updated, so exact records are not available to show the last visits to works of these locomotives.

Repairs were also carried out at the following (usually casual or light repairs).

Ashford
Brighton
Caerphilly
Cowlairs (Glasgow)
Eastleigh
Gorton
Newton Abbot
St Rollox (Glasgow)
Stratford.
Oswestry works (No. 70026 *Polar Star* was seen in March 1961)

It was more expedient to send the locomotives to the nearest works for this type of work than send them a long distance to Crewe, Swindon or Doncaster. Also some work could be carried out at larger sheds such as London (Old Oak Common) and Cardiff (Canton). No. 70004 *William Shakespeare* was in fact the last locomotive repaired at Darlington works, site when collision damage was completed in February 1965.

WITHDRAWALS

The first 'Britannia' to be withdrawn was No. 70007 *Coeur-de-Lion* in 1965. This was surprisingly early and probably resulted from a major problem. Previously the locomotive received a number of mainframe fractures (1961 and 1962) and had been a regular visitor at Doncaster works. Other early withdrawals include: No. 70017 *Arrow*,

involved in an accident on 3 August 1966 and withdrawn on 1 October 1966.

In October 1965 No. 70037 *Hereward the Wake* had a coupling rod fracture which pierced the boiler. There followed a long period in store at Carlisle (Kingmoor) with the rear driving wheels removed (the damage to the foot plating and boiler cladding was visible). No. 70037 was finally withdrawn on 5 November 1966, but was not scrapped until February 1968.

Withdrawals during the mid-1960s would be usually driven by condition or accident damage as the class was still required by the London Midland Region to perform Class 1 duties until 1967.

The last tranche of withdrawals occurred in December 1967 when all the remaining 'Britannias', except No. 70013 *Oliver Cromwell*, were withdrawn with the closure of Carlisle (Kingmoor) shed.

It was fitting that the last steam-hauled train on the British Railways network should be hauled by a 'Britannia' (No. 70013 *Oliver Cromwell*).

DISPOSALS

The class was unusual in that only one locomotive was scrapped at a BR works (No. 70007 *Coeur-de-Lion*). By the time that

the 'Britannias' were being disposed of BR had decided to sell locomotives to private scrap merchants. As the bulk of the class were allocated to Carlisle (Kingmoor) when withdrawn all were disposed of to scrap merchants in the locality, hence the number going to ship breakers in Scotland. Locomotives were scrapped at the following locations:

Crewe: No. 70007
Motherwell Machinery & Scrap Co. Ltd: Nos. 70001, 70018, 70027, 70036 and 70054.
West of Scotland Shipbreaking, Troon Harbour: No. 70019.
Cambell's Airdrie, Lanarks: Nos. 70002, 70003, 70005, 70008, 70025, 70033, 70046, 70047, 70050 and 70052.
Wards, Kilmarsh, Sheffield: Nos. 70023 and 70024.
Wards, Inverkeithing: Nos. 70004, 70014, 70021, 70022 and 70035.
Wards, Beighton, Sheffield: Nos. 70012, 70030, 70043, 70044 and 70045.
Cashmore, Newport: No. 70017 (damaged front end) and No. 70026
McWilliams, Shettleson, Glasgow: Nos. 70006, 70009, 70010, 70011, 70015, 70016, 70020, 70028, 70029, 70031, 70032, 70034, 70037, 70038, 70039, 70040, 70041, 70042, 70048, 70049, 70051 and 70053

Right:
No.70025 *Western Star*, at Greenholm in September 1967, still steam tight and in good enough condition to haul an express over Shap summit unaided. (CR/RPJ)

Below:
No.70050 *Firth of Clyde*, at Perth shed in 1962, fitted to a BR1D tender. The centre axle on the tender has been removed for repair. (CR/ HMR)

Left:
No. 70025 *Western Star*, near Preston, April 1965. The locomotive is absolutely filthy, but is running an express service. WR-style smoke deflectors are fitted. Despite its filthy condition it is still steam tight. No AWS or speedometer fitted. (DC)

Below:
No. 70025 *Western Star* at Shrewsbury shed (displaying the Western Region reporting number) presumably having worked up from Cardiff with a service that usually continued to Manchester via Crewe. No. 70025 is fitted with a battery box under the cab for the ATC equipment. (DC)

Left:
No. 70053 *Moray Firth* on a Kingswear-Wolverhampton train at Cheltenham, 28 August 1965. This locomotive was temporarily allocated to Wolverhampton (Oxley) along with two other 'Britannias' specifically to work Wolverhampton to the South Coast summer specials. (Note the 2B shed code on smokebox.) (IA)

Left:
No. 70041 *Sir John Moore* at Kings Cross when the locomotive had been re-allocated to Immingham (Grimsby) shed and used on the Cleethorpes-London service between 1961 and 1963. The Immingham allocation allowed an accelerated service and replaced the 'B1' class locomotives previously used. Once the allocation was increased to seven 'Britannias' there was a large enough 'pool' to run this accelerated service successfully. (DC)

Above:
No. 70003 *John Bunyan* at Chelmsford with the 07.45 Norwich to Liverpool Street London express service in December 1959. (CR/AC)

Left:
No. 70048 *The Territorial Army 1908-1958* at Edge Hill (Liverpool) shed, April 1963. Note the additional tank for the AWS mounted on the footplate. The nameplate was cast aluminium, the only one in this metal to be fitted on the class. No. 70048 has original-type smoke deflectors and LMS-style four-bolt fixing to the return crank. (IA/JC)

Left:
No. 70010 *Owen Glendower* at Stamford Town, Lincolnshire, in April 1962 on a Peterborough to Leicester local service. (CR/PHW)

CHAPTER FIVE

THE CLANS

The 'Clan' class spent most of the time in service
working on routes where its weight advantage was of
no benefit and was very much a 'general use' locomotive,
as likely to be seen on freight services as passenger traffic.

Even after the passing of 50 years it is still unclear why the 'Clan' class locomotives were built. Only 10 were constructed (below) from an original order of 25 and even after they were introduced it was not clear what they were intended for.

Being consistent to BR's standardisation ethos, the class shared many components with the 'Britannia' such as frames, tenders and many components of the running gear, the only items being unique to the class were the cylinders and boiler, resulting in a significant weight advantage the boiler being a smaller version of that on the 'Britannias' but with a lower boiler pressure at 225psi. The result was a neat looking locomotive

but which did not appear to offer any advantage over say an ex-LMS 'Jubilee' of similar power rating.

The class would have made sense if it could operate over routes with weight restrictions and was more powerful than the locomotives already in service. The 'Clan' class was rarely seen on the Highland main line to Inverness and except for the short period in 1956 was not used on the West Highland line. The 'Clan' class therefore spent most of the time in service working on routes where its weight advantage was of no benefit and was very much a 'general use' locomotive, as likely to be seen on freight services as passenger traffic.

BR Number	Name	Date Built	Original Tender	AWS	Speed Recorder	Withdrawn
No. 72000	Clan Buchanan	29/12/1951	BR1	Yes (02/1961)	02/1961	29/12/1962
No. 72001	Clan Cameron	29/12/1951	BR1	Yes (08/1959)	12/1958	29/12/1962
No. 72002	Clan Cambell	14/01/1952	BR1	Yes	5/1961	29/12/1962
No. 72003	Clan Fraser	19/01/1952	BR1	Yes (12/1960)	12/1960	29/12/1962
No. 72004	Clan MacDonald	02/02/1952	BR1	05/1960	12/61	29/12/1962
No. 72005	Clan MacGregor	19/02/1952	BR1	Never Fitted	Yes	01/05/1965
No. 72006	Clan MacKenzie	27/02/1952	BR1	08/1961	08/1961	21/05/1965
No. 72007	Clan MacKintosh	04/03/1952	BR1	Yes	Yes	04/12/1965
No. 72008	Clan MacLeod	14/03/1952	BR1	Yes	Yes	16/04/1966
No. 72009	Clan Stewart	26/03/1952	BR1	Yes	Yes	28/08/1965

Above:
No. 72006 *Clan MacKenzie* at Crewe works, 30 May 1954. The background colour to the nameplate is black. (CR)

Left:
No. 72001 *Clan Cameron* ready to depart Fort William with a train to Glasgow. The 'Clan' class was an unusual sight on this line, but this was in preparation for a special train for a reunion of the Clan Cameron in May 1956. (CR/KB)

Above:
No. 72004 *Clan MacGregor* at Carlisle (Kingmoor), May 1961. A speedometer is not fitted. The background colour to the nameplate is black. (CR/TO)

Right:
No. 72008 *Clan MacLeod* at Oxley (Wolverhampton) shed. The green painted cylinders are lined and the firebox cladding (below the footplate) is also green. The name-plate is finished with a red background. (CR)

CHANGES AND MODIFICATIONS

Unlike the 'Britannia' many of the small modifications such as the front steps and the fluted coupling rods remained as fitted.

Return Crank Fixing. As with the 'Britannia' the original LNER-style return crank fixing was changed to the LMS type with four stud fixing.

Smokebox Door Lamp Bracket. In 1963/64 the remaining members of the class (Nos. 72004/06/07/08/09) had the lamp bracket, at the top of the smokebox door, lowered to a position to the right of the smokebox door dart.

LIVERIES

The class received the same livery as the 'Britannia' but does not appear to have acquired the 'economy' green livery after the last major works attention in 1962. Also the 'Clans' were now the responsibility of Cowlairs Works who may have turned a blind

eye to instructions from Crewe. However at least one 'Clan' appears to have been 'patch' painted with the economy paint.

In August 1964 one of the class, No. 72006 *Clan MacKenzie*, was mistakenly painted with a yellow stripe through the number denoting that it was not to be used under the overhead wires south of Crewe.

Following overhaul in 1962 at Cowlairs works, No. 72009 *Clan Stewart* was observed with green (lined out) cylinders rather than the standard black.

The shed name was sometimes painted on the buffer beam with No. 72006 *Clan MacKenzie* seen with Carlisle (Kingmoor) in 1965.

At least one of the class, No. 72007 *Clan MacKintosh* had a red background to the smokebox number plate. This was seen when the locomotive was on a special working in 1964.

NAMES

Most of the 'Clans' appeared to have retained nameplates until withdrawal although No. 72006

Clan MacKenzie had lost the plates by May 1965. No. 72008 *Clan MacLeod* also had the nameplates removed in the same month.

ALLOCATION

When first built the class was split between two sheds, the first five going to Glasgow (Polmadie) and the second five were sent to Carlisle (Kingmoor) which at that time was part of the Scottish Region. At the time of withdrawal the class was as first allocated but in the intervening years a number of transfers took place. In October 1958 No. 72009 *Clan Stewart* was allocated to Stratford Depot in London for trials on the Great Eastern but was returned to Carlisle in December 1958. At various times between 1957 and 1959 the first six locomotives were re-allocated to Edinburgh (St Margarets) and Edinburgh (Haymarket) but all had returned to the original sheds between 1958 and 1960.

Above:
No. 72006 *Clan MacKenzie* at Farringdon Junction in 1964. Note the lowered top lamp bracket on the smokebox door. AWS equipment is fitted. (CR)

Left:
No. 70008 *Clan MacLeod* at Blackpool North, 27 September 1965. The nameplates have been removed and lining is visible on the edge of the footplate. The cabside appears to have been 'patch' painted in plain green. (DC)

ROUTES

Being allocated to Glasgow and Carlisle the class was common on the West Coast main line between Preston and Glasgow but was also seen regularly in Manchester and Blackpool. During the summer there were a large number of holiday specials from Glasgow to Blackpool and 'Clans' were regularly used.

The class was also regularly used on the former Glasgow & South Western route to Stranraer regularly working the boat trains.

When members of the class were transferred to Edinburgh they were used to replace 'V2' class 2-6-2 locomotives on passenger and freight workings over the Waverley route between Edinburgh and Carlisle.

When the class was reduced to five locomotives, Carlisle used them on a variety of duties and they were also in demand for working enthusiast specials. No. 72006 *Clan MacKenzie* was used by Old Oak Common in

December 1963 for a special train from Paddington to Swindon and return. Old Oak did a good job of cleaning the locomotive as it had arrived from the north in a filthy state.

Sightings of 'Clans' at locations not normally associated with the class almost became a sport in the 1960s with locomotives being seen at Shrewsbury, Bristol, Sheffield and Huddersfield also at the the southern end of the Midland mainline. Late in service the

'Carlisle Five' were regularly used on the Settle and Carlisle route and on all types of working to Leeds and Bradford.

WORKS

When first built the class was maintained at Crewe works but from 1962 responsibility passed to St Rollox and Cowlairs and then solely to Cowlairs.

WITHDRAWAL AND DISPOSAL

The first five locomotives (all at Glasgow Polmadie) were all withdrawn at the end of December 1962 and stored. Eventually all were moved to Darlington works by September 1963 and remained there until early 1964 before being scrapped.

The Carlisle (Kingmoor) allocation carried on working until May 1965 when No. 72005 *Clan MacGregor* was withdrawn and following the trend at that time was delivered to the scrapyard of Arnott Young at Troon, Ayrshire, for cutting up.

By the end of 1965 only one locomotive remained and No. 72008 *Clan MacLeod* continued in service until April 1966 before being withdrawn. It was delivered to McWilliams at Shettleston, central Glasgow, for cutting up in June 1966. None survived into preservation.

CHAPTER SIX

PRESERVATION

Only two 'Britannias' have been preserved
and both are soon to be restored to full operating
condition for the benefit of future enthusiasts.

Although it was always certain that one of the class would be preserved, it is surprising that, given a sizable number of the class survived until the end of 1967, other examples were not saved. However many of the early preservation schemes were more interested in smaller (and to them) more practicable locomotives and none of the 'Britannias' made it to the haven of the Barry scrap yard in South Wales where it could be rescued at a later date.

In the end the fact that two were preserved was mainly as a result of a change of heart by the authorities as to which engine to retain.

The preserved locomotives are:

No. 70000 *Britannia*. Withdrawn in June 1966 and intended to be part of the National Collection but following a long period in storage the condition of the locomotive deteriorated to the point where its place in the National Railway Museum (NRM) was taken by No. 70013 *Oliver Cromwell*. Following this change of plan the locomotive was purchased by The Britannia Locomotive Group and moved to the Severn Valley Railway. It then moved to the Nene Valley Railway (near Peterborough). In the 1980s it was fitted with air pumps so that the locomotive could haul the air-braked Continental rolling stock used on the Nene Valley. No. 70000 was used to

work on the main line until major work was required and has been stored since the late 1990s, with ownership moving to Pete Waterman. The locomotive is now on static display at the Barrow Hill roundhouse. It has very recently (January 2006) been sold and the expectation is that it will be returned to steam which will lead to it being removed from Barrow Hill.

No. 70013 *Oliver Cromwell*. Following the last steam-hauled train on BR the locomotive (now part of the National Railway Museum collection) ran light to Diss, Norfolk, where it was transported by road to Alan Bloom's steam museum (Bressingham Gardens) set amongst his extensive nursery and gardens. No. 70013 was steamed but there was only a short length of track for running. Ownership of the locomotive was disputed between the NRM and the museum at Diss over the years but this was finally resolved in 2004 when it was moved to the Great Central Railway.

The locomotive is currently in a fully-dismantled condition in its workshops at Loughborough, Leicestershire, where No. 70013 is receiving a full overhaul ready for return to main-line working.

If more of the class had been sent to Barry some would have survived for restoration. As scrap value is rated in pounds-per-ton the scrapman's torch had little sympathy.

Above:
No. 70000 *Britannia* when running on the Nene Valley Railway. The locomotive is fitted with air pumps for hauling Continental (air-braked) stock. Note the additional air pipe on the buffer beam. (DC)

Left:
No. 70000 *Britannia* on the Nene Valley Railway, with the author's brother Phillip on fireman duties. (DC)

1951

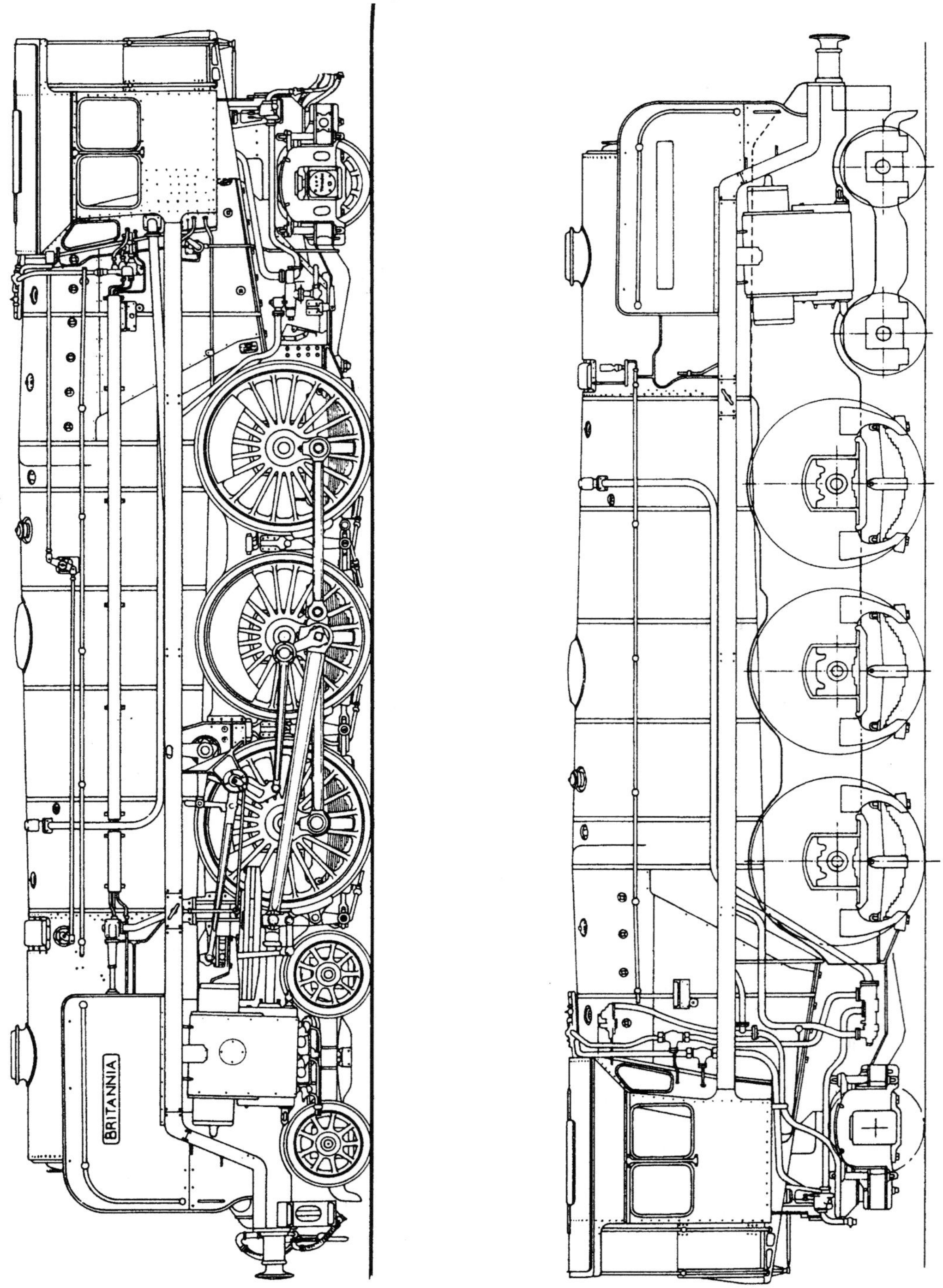

Class 7 'Britannia'

© Copyright 2006 Mike Peascod

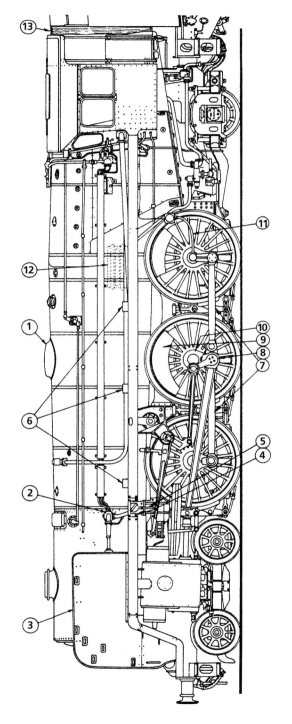

1   Dome.

2   Exhaust ejector. Following the accident at Milton a number of Western Region allocated locomotives had the ejector modified.

3   Smoke deflectors handholds.

4   Lubricator covers. On the first 25 locomotives the foot plating covered the front face of the mechanical lubricator. This was subsequently removed.

5   Lubricator drive rod. The lubricators were driven by a rod from the expansion link which pushed a vertical oscillating rod to the lubricator. As built the drive rod was parallel to the rails, but on a number of locomotives this was modified such that this rod then operated at an angle and the vertical rod shortened.

6   Sandbox lids.

7   Coupling rods.

8   Return crank fixing.

9   Driving wheel balance weights.

10 Coupled wheel axles.

11 Speedometers.

12 ATC/AWS equipment.

13 Draught curtain.

Class 7 'Britannia' Modifications

© Copyright 2006 Mike Peascod

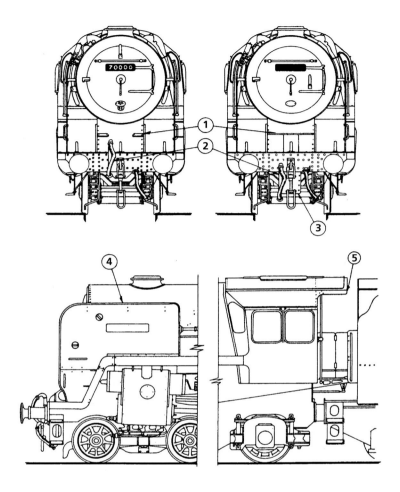

1   Smokebox footsteps.

2   Front vacuum brake pipes. As originally built the first 25 locomotives had vertical vacuum pipes and were above the buffer beam. The subsequent locomotives had the pipe emerging from the middle of the buffer beam. Most were modified.

3   ATC/AWS equipment.

4   Smoke deflectors handholds.

5   Cab back. Locomotives fitted with BR1/1A tenders had a vertical handrail at the back of the cab, those fited with BR1D did not, the handrail being on the tender.

Class 7 'Britannia' Modifications

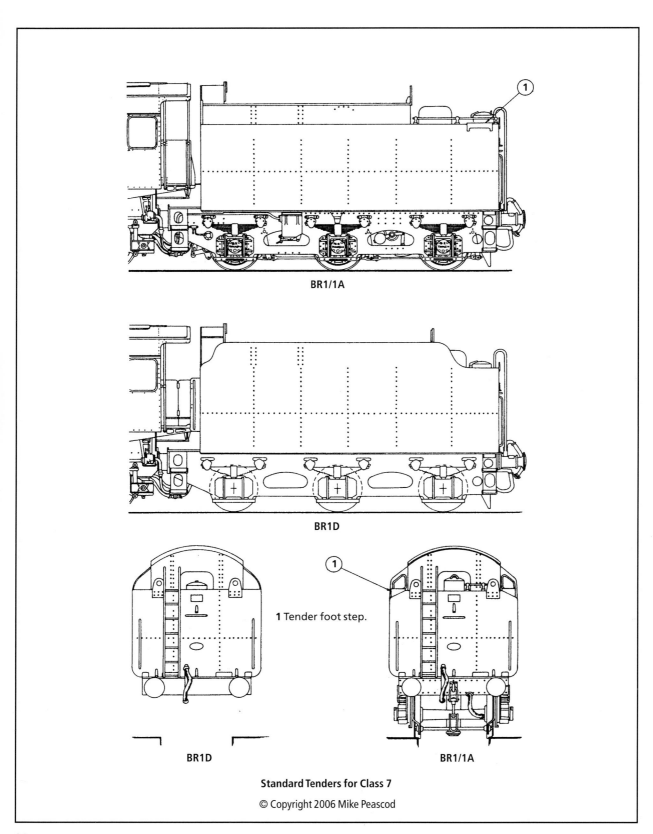

BR1/1A

BR1D

1 Tender foot step.

BR1D

BR1/1A

Standard Tenders for Class 7

© Copyright 2006 Mike Peascod

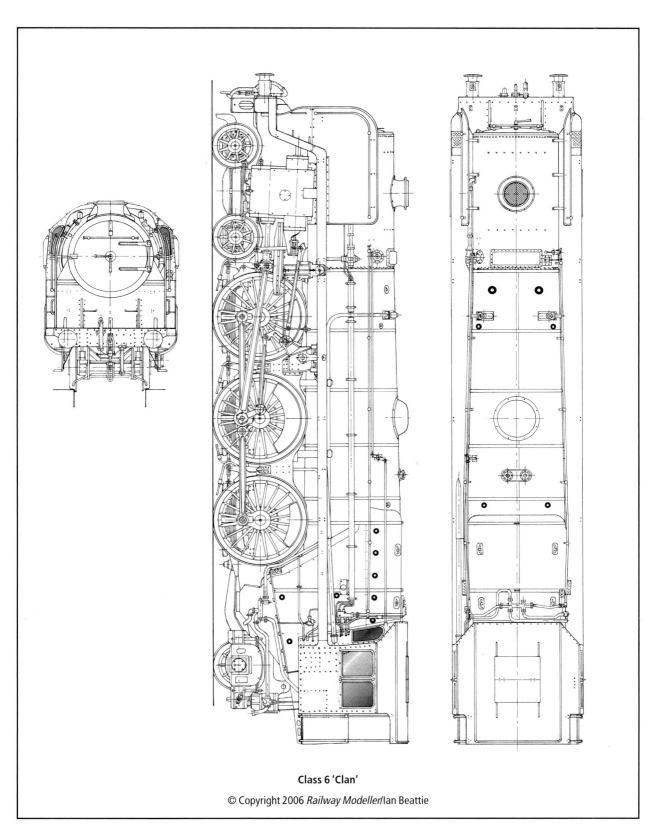

Class 6 'Clan'

© Copyright 2006 *Railway Modeller*/Ian Beattie

Above: No. 70016 *Ariel* with a banker at Greenholme in 1965. (CR/MC)